Amazing
HYPNOTHERAPY
Tales

MOSAICA PRESS

Amazing HYPNOTHERAPY *Tales*

HEALING WITH HYPNOSIS
THE **JEWISH** WAY

Bracha Pearl Toporowitch, CHT

ISBN: 978-1-952370-55-7

Published by Mosaica Press, Inc.
www.mosaicapress.com
info@mosaicapress.com

ADVANCE PRAISE

This is a must-read book if you want to understand how your subconscious mind works in health and sickness, written by a talented and highly professional hypnotherapist. You will gain insights into how you can heal, physically, emotionally or spiritually by activating the Mind-Body connection. The science and art of hypnotherapy is truly amazing, accomplishing often what conventional healing cannot accomplish. You will be astounded by what you read in this book and it can help you to achieve true healing. I would highly recommend it for both professionals and lay people.

Efim Svirsky, founder and director of The Institute of Jewish Spiritual Therapy, hypnotherapist, educator, and author of Connection

In Bracha Toporowitch's book *Amazing Hypnotherapy Tales*, we glimpse the world of hypnotherapy and its incredible power. Bracha's years of training and experience with hypnosis, which works faster and goes deeper than guided imagery, enable her to achieve remarkable results in amazingly short periods of time. The Torah world can gain greatly from taking advantage of this non-invasive modality, with virtually no side effects, for physical-mental-emotional-spiritual healing. Compare this to conventional healing, which treats the body alone, or talk therapies, dealing mostly with the conscious mind. The practical tools at the end make the book so much more valuable!

I enjoyed every page, and I came away inspired by the wonders Hashem implanted within us and with what can be achieved by the skillful use of those wonders. I recommend reading this book to anyone in need of healing or wishing to discover the power of the mind.

Chaya Hinda Allen, Guided Imagery practitioner

Bracha Toporowitch has written a very interesting book describing her experience as a hypnotherapist. The book shows how useful hypnotherapy can be by detailing cases of people whom she has helped. This is a technique that can boost confidence and assist in overcoming many inner challenges, and I think any intelligent reader will see its benefits when responsibly administered.

Rabbi Dr. Akiva Tatz, world-renowned lecturer and author; founder, Jewish Medical Ethics Forum

In loving memory

I dedicate this book to my father-in-law
L'ilui nishmas

הגה״צ ר׳ שלמה בן יצחק לייב הלוי, זצ״ל

RAV SHLOMO HALEVI TOPOROWITCH, ZT"L

and my mother-in-law
L'ilui nishmas

הרבנית תהלה בת ר׳ יחזקאל משה הלוי, ז״ל

RABBANIT TEHILLA (BORNSTEIN) TOPOROWITCH, Z"L

Through their *mesirus nefesh,* despite great deprivation, they implanted a pure Torah education in their children. And through their relentless toil, they successfully planted Torah in a spiritual desert. The fruit of their labor is a beacon of light until today, spreading Hakadosh Baruch Hu's illumination in the world.

יהי זכרם ברוך

DEDICATED BY FRIENDS AND STUDENTS

Wishing you much *berachah* and *hatzlachah*
in your work and in all your endeavors.

L'ilui nishmas

רייצא בת אברהם בונם ז״ל

דוד דניאל בן אריה לייב ז״ל

סימה איטא בת דוב בער ז״ל

ברוך בן אברהם ז״ל

In loving memory from their children and grandchildren

L'refuah sheleimah v'yeshuos

CHAYA KREINDEL BAS RUDA, TICHYEH

L'ilui nishmas

DON ZEVULUN BEN REUVEN, Z"L

Rabbi Zev Leff

הרב זאב לף

Rabbi of Moshav Matityahu
Rosh HaYeshiva—Yeshiva Gedola Matityahu

מרא דאתרא מושב מתתיהו
ראש הישיבה—ישיבה גדולה מתתיהו

D.N. Modiin 71917   **Tel:** 08-976-1138 'טל   **Fax:** 08-976-5326 'פקס   ד.נ. מודיעין 71917

Dear Friends,

Rabbeinu Yonah in *Shaarei Teshuvah* (*shaar* 3, number 71) mandates that every community should have people trained to help men and women who are in distress as a fulfillment of "*Lo sa'amod al dam reyecha*—Do not stand idly by when your neighbor is in danger."

It may seem strange to see a rabbinical approbation on this book, *Amazing Hypnotherapy Tales*, by Mrs. Bracha Toporowitch. However, after having seen approbations from esteemed Rabbanim as to the caliber of Mrs. Toporowitch as a true woman of valor, a woman imbued with Torah values and fear of heaven, who has benefited countless women through her expertise as a certified hypnotherapist, I feel that this book will encourage those who can be helped through this method to seek aid. Additionally, this work can inspire others to pursue a similar course to become hypnotherapists to follow in Mrs. Toporowitch's footsteps in meriting the community.

I pray that Hashem Yisborach reward Mrs. Toporowitch for her aid to the community and bless her and her family with life, health, and all the Heavenly blessings.

Sincerely,

With Torah blessings

Zev Leff

Rabbi Zev Leff

Rabbi MOSHE NACHSHONI
12 HARAV KOOK st

הרב משה נחשוני
רח' הרב קוק 12 ראשון לציון
טלפון: 03-9648512
נייד:054-8481181

ח/חשון/תשפ"א

בס"ד

מרת ברכה פרל טופרוביץ אשת הרבני התורני הר"ר
יחזקאל זכתה לרפא רבים ע"י היפנותרפיה, גם ממחלות
קשות שאין להם פיתרון בשלימות ע"י רפואת רגילות.
היא מוסמכת בהפינוזה, וזה למעלה מעשרים שנה היא
מצליחה מאד, וראיתי עדויות מאנשים שנושעו ע"י בדרך
זאת,וידוע פסקו של פוסק הדור הגאון ר' משה פיינשטיין
זצ"ל שצירף לפסקו גם את הגאון הרב העצנקין זצ"ל שאין
שום איסור בשיטת ריפוי זאת, ועכשיו היא הוציאה ספר
המסביר חשיבות הטיפול הזה שבנוי שהגוף תלוי בנפש
וכל טיפול מתאים בנפש עוזר לגוף, והאמת ששלמה
המלך החכם מכל אדם כתב יסוד זה [משלי י"ח,
י"ד],,רוח איש יכלכל מחלהו,, ורש"י מפרש שרוח גבר
שאין לו דאגה יכלכל מחלהו שאין כוחו סר ממנו. וראיתי
יסוד זה גם על בשרי. ע"כ הנני ממליץ לקנות הספר.
אמנם איני מכיר את צדדי הריפוי רק בכלליות, וגם לא
עברתי על פרטיו, אולם משפחת טופורוביץ היא משפחה
רבנית ותורנית ידועה וגם האדמו"ר מחוסט שליט"א
שיבחם מאד וגם יש הסכמה מהגאון הרב לף שליט"א.
והספר יעזור לרבים. ע"כ הנני מצטרף להסכמה
הכותב לטובת הציבור

הרב משה נחשוני ראשל"צ

משה נחשוני

הרב משה נחשוני
רחי הרב קוק 12
ראשון-לציון
03-9648512 טל 03-9648512

Rabbi Reuven T. Pozen
Rav of KEHILA CHAREDIT
Zichron Yakov.
Tel.:03-5794956

הרב ראובן טוביה פוזן
מ״מ רב הקהילה החרדית בזכרון יעקב
כתובת: רח׳ נחמיה 19 בני ברק
טל׳: 03-5794956

בס״ד   אייר תשנ״ה

אני הח״מ מכיר את משפחת גרי יתכאל מאשראשיל
כי זאנהו שהם הרבה טובוטורוים את״ ש״וואהן ר״שים
לוצאי ל״ען שלם זה כאן ר״שים ולא כדיג יש לי״ם ע״ם
הורה ב״ל״הד,

הנ״ז ל״ל הכ״ב ו״ראא כ״ין ו״אבא, ל״מש על״ה,

 דבר כן,

ואשן ס, כ/ן
מ״ז ג׳קה״לה ה״חרדית
ב״כ״ון י״ל״ל

הנני ב״ל״ל ל״לל ב״אר ל״שח ס״וורי״א ל״וורו״ג״ו
אה״ר״ו״ו״ו ל״של״ם וום ל״ר״ש״ח ל״ל״ל״ל״ו ל״ל״ל״ו ל״ר״ש״ח
ה״ו ר״ש ל״ל ו״ש״ו״ו   ל״ל״ל״ו

י״ל ר״״ל

דוד רייכמן

Rabbi Rephoel Szmerla
1447 Monmouth Avenue
Lakewood, NJ 08701

רפאל שמערלא
מו״ץ בבית הוראה דליקוואוד
שבנשיאות מורנו הרה״ג רב שלמה אליהו מילר שליט״א
מחו״ס יכי אני ה׳ רופאך׳ על רפואה אלטרנטיבית בהלכה

I have seen Mrs. Toporowitch's compilation of real-life stories of healing through hypnotherapy. Her goal was to illustrate the many conditions treatable through hypnotherapy, so that those who could benefit from it will know where to turn. Thus, she has done a great service to the *tsibbur* by presenting this form of therapy and explaining its great potential.

Hypnotism is a way to access the subconscious, and hypnotherapists use it to correct many types of emotional and psychological issues, as well as physical ailments that have an emotional component at their core - psychosomatic illnesses. Treating ailments of this nature is known as "Mind-Body Healing" and is an important aspect of hypnotherapy.

As I have explained in my *sefer*, accessing the subconscious is certainly permitted, as long as it is not done for the purpose of divining the future. As a result, hypnotherapy is unquestionably permitted. It was first discussed 150 years ago by the *Aruch L'ner* and *Maharsham*, who permitted it. More recently, *Hagaon Rav Yosef Eliyahu Henkin, Hagaon Rav Moshe Feinstein, Hagaon Rav Shmuel Wosner zt'l* and *Hagaon Rav Mordechai Gross shlita* also ruled that the use and practice of hypnotherapy is permitted.

As with all psychotherapists, one must ensure to enlist the help of a hypnotherapist who is not only *shomer Torah uMitsvos* but also whose *haskafah* is completely in line with *Daas Torah*. I am confident that Mrs. Toporowitch fulfills these requirements. May she merit that her book be influential in popularizing hypnotherapy in *klal Yisrael*.

Rabbi Rephoel Szmerla, Lakewood, NJ

R' ARYEH NIVIN'S
PERSONAL DEVELOPMENT CHABURAS

Aryeh Nivin
HaPalmach 33/1
Ashdod, Israel 77376
Chaburapa@gmail.com

Rosh Chodesh Kislev 5781

As a coach and a teacher of Personal Development for over 35 years I am keenly aware of how a person's beliefs, emotions, and past traumas affect a person's life for the good and the bad.

While reading Mrs Toporowitch's work about hypnotherapy I was reminded of the extent of the mind to heal, not only the emotions and the spirit of the client, but the physical body as well.

I have read sections of this work. This book gives the reader a fascinating glimpse into the person's inner world, the subconscious mind.

I recommend this book to anyone who wants to understand the mind-body connection and how it can enable one to achieve health, happiness and well-being.

R. Aryeh Leib Dovid Nivin

אי רה ניזין

TABLE OF CONTENTS

PREFACE

I discovered the power of hypnosis when I was a patient at a pain clinic, being treated for the pain syndrome known as fibromyalgia, for which conventional medicine has no known cure. Hypnosis was one of the therapies I used. It allowed me to understand that many of our ailments do not stem only from physical sources, but other elements, such as emotions, beliefs, preconceived ideas about life, and ingrained habits affect our physical body as well. I came to know that we are a mind and a body, and one influences the other. As the intensity of my pain lessened and my life changed during the time I was treated in that clinic, I uncovered a whole new world called "mind-body healing."

I became fascinated with this new world and wanted to know more. For many years, I had worked with women in various capacities, such as childbirth preparation and lactation consulting, and I realized that here was an amazing tool I could add to my "toolbox." Before long, I took the necessary courses and in 1999 became certified in hypnosis.

After taking my initial course with the International Association of Counselors and Therapists in New York, I studied with the National Guild of Hypnotists in New Hampshire, and then with British Hypnosis Research in London. More recently, I became a member of the American Hypnosis Association and continue to broaden my education. Over the years, I have accumulated a vast body of knowledge in how to use hypnosis for myriad issues. One of my favorite areas is Hypno-Fertility, using hypnosis for fertility issues. On my journey I learned Hypno-Oncology and had the privilege of helping women suffering with cancer.

I practiced the art of hypnosis with women and girls in religious communities in several countries, on three continents. I have worked with thousands of clients over the years in private sessions, in group settings, and in workshops. My experiences were extremely gratifying—and usually very effective, despite the fact that on occasion, I was not able to achieve the desired outcome for a particular client. Even in those situations, the hypnosis we did helped her in some other way.

During my years of therapeutic work with women, I was deeply troubled by the fact that so many of my clients, young and old, were plagued with irrational fears and phobias. This malady not only affected their emotional well-being, but it often impacted their physical health and even their spirituality. Many expressed their inability to daven and connect to Hashem in a loving relationship, as a result of their suffering. I knew I had a powerful tool that could help alleviate this sad situation.

And so, dear readers, my goal in recording some of these hypnosis sessions is not simply to give you a good read, but to reveal to you the power of the mind, and to remind us all never to underestimate it. The Gemara in *Makkos* (10b) says: *"B'derech she'adam rotzeh leilech bah molichin oso*—The path on which one wishes to travel, on that path will they lead him." The words *"molichin oso"* mean, "they" lead him. But who are "they"? Who or what is the entity that brings a person to that road that he chooses to go down?

The *Maharsha* answers that every time a person has a desire or a thought, he creates a *malach*, a supernatural force. A good thought creates a good *malach*; a bad thought, a bad *malach*. It is those *malachim* that are created through our thoughts that are *"molichin oso,"* bringing a person down the road he wishes to traverse.

We can utilize this power to be led down the road of healing. Hypnosis is a powerful way of accomplishing this. The healing we achieve can be in the body, the intellect, the emotions, and in the spirit. Sometimes, the transformations I have been privy to participate in have been so startling that I began to truly understand the well-known quote of Mark Twain, "Truth is stranger than fiction."

My accounts of these therapy sessions are not verbatim. However, from my thorough notes on the sessions and from the audio recordings of the hypnotic trances I have done, I have been able to faithfully reconstruct these true accounts. Often, I explain why I did or said certain things in the hypnotherapy sessions so that the reader can understand the rationale behind them. I did not necessarily share these insights with my clients, but I have included them for the benefit of the reader. Obviously, the names of my clients and any doctors mentioned have been changed, as well as some identifying details, in order to protect the privacy of the individuals involved. In a few cases, I combined several clients into a composite person, her tale telling the story of a few.

With these stories, I aim to show the numerous ways hypnosis has been able to change a person's life for the better. However, I strongly caution my readers not to utilize this therapy on their own, unless they have been professionally trained in its use. Hypnotherapy is both a science and an art. It takes much learning and training and some more learning and training, and—no less important—the training must take place through moral and upright individuals. Of course, it goes without saying, if a halachic or *hashkafic* concern was to arise, the trainee would seek the counsel of *daas Torah*. Additionally, it requires lots of practice under the watchful eye of a skilled professional hypnotist to hone your own skills. Those who put in the required time and effort to be properly trained, with *siyata d'Shmaya*, will be able to achieve their own amazing hypnotherapy tales.

That being said, I'd like to add that after studying the contents of these stories the reader will be able to utilize the many non-hypnosis self-help tools and techniques I have described in great detail. And, in order to make these exercises more user-friendly, I have included an appendix in which I teach the reader when and how to use some simple but powerful "non-hypnosis" techniques.

So, settle down comfortably and get ready to embark on an amazing journey into the deepest recesses of the inner mind!

Bracha Pearl Toporowitch, CHT
Zichron Yaakov, Teves 5781 / January 2021

ACKNOWLEDGMENTS

I send to You, Hakadosh Boruch Hu, my overwhelming gratitude for giving me the words which enabled me to write this book. To You, my Creator, I express my heartfelt thanks for giving me the skills needed to treat the people I wrote about. And, Ribbono Shel Olam, despite the inconvenience, I appreciate the lockdown You arranged for me, so that I had the necessary time and space in which to write.

To my dear family, you believed in me and gave me the support I needed to create this work, I give my loving and ongoing thanks.

To my dear daughters, Chana and Tehilla, *tichyu*, my deep-felt appreciation and thanks for giving freely of your time in reviewing the manuscript again and once again, as well as for your perceptive insights and suggestions for improvement.

To the wonderful members of the Mosaica Press team who brought this book to publication, crafted professionally and beautifully, I give you my sincere thanks. And to the gifted graphic artists, Rayzel Broyde and the rest of the team, who created an exquisite book cover, a work of artistry, piquing the curiosity of the reader to discover what lies within, I send my deepest appreciation.

To my editors at Mosaica Press, Rabbi Doron Kornbluth, Sherie Gross, and the entire editing staff, once again, I deeply thank you for your expertise and skill in refining and enhancing this work. It was a pleasure working with you.

To my numerous teachers and mentors in the field of hypnosis and mind-body healing, contributing to my knowledge and skills, each in their own way, I send my boundless thanks. Learning from many of you directly, and from some indirectly, was an amazing experience. I wish to thank each individually:

Milton H. Erickson, M.D., creator of Ericksonian Indirect Hypnosis

Stephen Brooks, PsyD, hypnotherapist, Founder and Director of British Hypnosis Research

Paul Aurand, MHt, Founder and Director of the Holistic Healing Center in New York City

Roy Hunter, MS FAPHP, Parts Therapy

Ron Eslinger, RN, BCH (Board Certified Hypnotherapist), Pain Management

Marilyn Gordon, BCH, Transformational Healing

Lynsi Eastburn, BCH, Hypnofertility[R]

Sjanie H. Wurlitzer, D.Hyp, The Fertile Body Method

Rev. Scot Giles, BCH, Hypno-Oncology, Complementary Medical Hypnotism

John Melton, CHT, Hypnosis and Tinnitus, Hypnosis and Pain Management

Lisa Machenberg, CHT, PTSD Healing

Cheryl O'Neil, CHT, Healing the Inner Child

John Kappas, Ph.D. Founder of the Hypnosis Motivation Institute and the American Hypnosis Association

Bernie Siegel, M.D.

Alice Domar, M.D.

Kevin Hogan, Ph.D.

Martin Rossman, M.D.

Belleruth Naparstek, PsyD.

And last, but certainly not least, to my students and clients, I profoundly thank you from the bottom of my heart for putting your trust in me. You give me the ability to learn how to interact with people with discernment, as each is a world unto herself. Every one of you was another part of the journey in my becoming the hypnotherapist that I am today.

INTRODUCTION

MIND-BODY HEALING:
THE POWER OF IMAGINATION AND HYPNOSIS

Part I: The Torah Approach

The following is a loose translation of the Hebrew, written by Yisrael Halevi Toporowitch, author of Derech Yisrael, Rosh Kollel of Amal HaTorah, Achisamach; Rav of Kehillas Chazon Ish, Achisamach and Beit Shemesh; Rav of Beit Knesset Ohel Leah, Beit Shemesh. The original Hebrew text appears in Appendix E.

In terms of the mind physically influencing the body, I can't say that I understand how the mind physically influences the body. However, we find that Yaakov Avinu put the [specially prepared] sticks in the water troughs. *Midrash Tanchuma* 7 on *Parashas Naso* brings the following story: The king of the Arabs said to Rabbi Akiva, "I'm a black man and my wife is black and she gave birth to a white child..." Rabbi Akiva told him that his wife had focused on a white form, and "if this phenomenon astounds you, you can learn from Yaakov Avinu's sheep that conceived from the sticks" [i.e., they bore sheep with similar markings as were engraved on the sticks]. The Arab king thanked Rabbi Akiva and praised him.

The *Ramban* in *Parashas Chukas* writes—calling it one of the marvels of cause and effect—that if someone was bitten by a rabid dog, after he becomes ill, when his urine is put in a glass vessel, one can see figures of small puppies in the urine. If the urine is poured through a cloth to filter it, there will be no impressions on the cloth. When the urine is returned to the glass vessel and allowed to settle for a while, once again, the small puppy figures will reappear in the urine. The *Ramban* writes that this is a true phenomenon, and it is one of the wonders of the spiritual powers.

The following is a loose translation of the Hebrew, written by Dovid Halevi Toporowitch, author of Divrei Moshe. The original Hebrew text appears in Appendix E.

A. It is written in *Parashas Bereishis* (2:7): "And G-d formed man of earth from the ground, and He breathed into his nostrils the soul of life, and man became a living soul." One of the greatest mysteries and wonders of creation is the human being. As long as the soul of life is in the body, Hashem created an inseparable bond of spirituality and physicality. This is a miracle and a mystery. This connection is not merely that the physical body can operate in spiritual ways, but that the physical has the ability to affect the spirit and that the spirit has the ability to affect the physical. A simple example of this is, "And wine will make a human heart rejoice" (*Tehillim* 14:15). We are used to the idea that when alcohol enters the blood it affects the person. But actually, this thing is a wonder—that wine, which is physical, can affect the emotions, which are spiritual.

There are interactions between the body and the mind that people are generally aware of and recognize as true, for example, that mental stress greatly affects the body and can cause illness and pain, G-d forbid. Although stress is an emotion and part of man's spiritual makeup, it has the ability to affect the physical body in many ways. It is also common knowledge that joy can affect the body in down-regulating pain and in healing. This is stated explicitly in *Mishlei* (17:22): "A merry heart enhances healing..." Rabbeinu Yonah writes there that the joy of the heart is the reason a person heals from his illness. Naturally, there are less widely known phenomena that the Sages discuss.

B. There are two mental and spiritual forces that can physically affect the body. The first is the emotions, such as happiness, sadness, anger, etc. The second is the imagination and thoughts. We read in *Mishlei* (15:30): "And good news fattens the bones" and (17:22): "But a broken spirit dries the bones" (see the commentators there). On *Mishlei* (15:13), "A merry heart makes a cheerful countenance," Rabbeinu Yonah writes that Shlomo HaMelech wants us to learn that **the heart has an effect on the body because most of the pleasure and the distress of the body depend on the heart.**

In *Gittin* 51b, Rabbi Yochanan ben Zakai came to the Roman general who was about to capture Jerusalem. After the general had put on one shoe, he received news that he had been appointed emperor over Rome. He was then unable to put on his second shoe and could not remove the shoe he was wearing. Rabbi Yochanan explained that this was because of the good news he had just received. His advice was to bring someone the general hated into his presence, and after doing so, he was able to put on his second shoe.

C. The Torah illustrates the great influence of thought and imagination on the body in the story of Yaakov

Avinu and his sheep, as mentioned above. The *Midrash Rabbah* (73:10) on this story brings another incident that further illustrates the point.

A black man was married to a black woman, who gave birth to a white child, as mentioned above.

With these illustrations, Chazal teach us that the power of thought and visualization can cause animals to give birth to offspring different from their normal color and, likewise, black parents can give birth to a white child. The *Ramban* writes at length in *Igros Hakodesh*, chapter 5, of how much power and influence and strength are embedded in thoughts and imagery. He elaborates along these lines on the subject of the copper snake in *Parashas Chukas* (21:9).

D. Everyone has two "minds"—the conscious mind and the subconscious mind. Simply said, the conscious mind makes judgments and deliberates, and engages in all the things we refer to as intelligence. The subconscious mind acts automatically, utilizing reflexes, instincts, and so on. Both minds have their merits and flaws, and we need both in order to exist. All of a person's memories from the moment of conception are stored in the subconscious mind. Oftentimes, the conscious mind does not have access to this database, which is stored in the area of the brain that is below the conscious level. In hypnosis, in a trance state, the subconscious mind can be accessed. Hypnotherapists, as well as doctors and psychologists, use hypnosis as a tool to uncover the hidden causes of distress or illness and then guide the subconscious mind to neutralize them.

E. The *hashkafah* of my mother, *ad meah v'esrim shanah*, relating to mind-body healing, is that Hashem can do anything, He is the ultimate Healer, and she is merely His messenger. Her goal is to help people via her vast stores of knowledge accumulated over years, and to impart to her clients that there are alternate ways of healing other than the conventional ones. Chazal (*Yerushalmi, Kesubos* 13b) say that not from everyone can a person become healed. My mother believes that her knowledge and experience create the pipeline through which Hashem sends healing to her clients.

F. The following are sources for halachic rulings dealing with hypnotherapy, guided imagery, and the like. Rav Yaakov Ettlinger, author of *Aruch L'Ner*, in *Responsa Binyan Tzion* (1:67), rules that hypnosis is permissible, as does Rav Moshe Feinstein in his responsa *Igros Moshe*, *Y.D.* (3:44).

I cannot give my opinion on the various forms of medicine that exist today, but in relation to the methods that my mother uses, it is simple to say that they are permissible according to halachah because she does not use any form of mystical healing, such as incantations. She uses her knowledge and experience to influence the body and the emotions, primarily through the medium of thoughts and visualization.

One can be deeply pained that many people and doctors, and even many *rabbanim*, are not familiar with the concept of mind-body healing. How sad it is that people spend small fortunes and countless years going from doctor to doctor in search of their "cure." Only after exhausting all options and giving up hope do they decide to try some form of mind-body healing. And then, surprisingly, they experience their great "miracle" for which they were waiting and praying for years.

Over the years, I heard from my mother many hard-to-believe stories of healing and salvation. But rather than relating a secondhand tale, I will relate a story that I was involved in. My wife and I know a family in which the mother gave birth to several children and then became infertile for several years. We suggested she see my mother and after a series of sessions, she became pregnant. From both the patient and the practitioner we learned that the woman had undergone a major emotional upheaval, and this had interfered with her ability to conceive. After the problem was addressed, *b'chasdei Hashem*, she became pregnant and bore a healthy child.

Part II: The Scientific Approach

Most people will readily agree that we are a mind-body, which means that the mind has the ability to affect the body and the body can affect the mind. A simple example of the mind affecting the body might be that when reading a scary story, one's heart begins beating faster. How might a person's body affect his mind? A child born with a disability that leaves him wheelchair bound feels sad and depressed and he might believe that he is a failure. When someone imagines something vividly, his brain believes it to be real and responds accordingly. Imagining biting into a lemon will almost always cause a person to salivate. His brain is responding to the picture in his mind as though it were true.

In part I, we read words from Torah sources stating, for example, that happiness brings healing and hating causes the bones to dry up. Hashem created humans with numerous interactions between mind and body and the more we understand them, the more we can benefit from them.

The emotions profoundly affect our health. The neglect of the mind-body connection by Westernized modern medicine is actually a recent phenomenon. Until the nineteenth century, medical people constantly paid attention to the influence of grief, despair, or discouragement on the onset and outcome of illness. Likewise, they did not ignore the healing effects of faith, confidence, and peace of mind. It is true that the modern man of medicine has gained much control over certain diseases through drugs; however, he has forgotten about the potential strength that exists within the patient.

Scientists have studied the phenomenon of the mind-body connection in depth and developed techniques for using it for healing, whether physically, mentally, emotionally, or spiritually. One of these techniques is hypnosis, whereby the hypnotherapist accesses deeper levels of the mind and activates responses that bring about healing.

Our mind is comprised of the conscious mind and the subconscious mind (sometimes referred to as the unconscious mind). It is believed that the conscious is approximately 5 percent of our mind, while the subconscious comprises 95 percent of it. There are many areas under the jurisdiction of the subconscious mind; functions that take no conscious thought or intervention, such as digestion, breathing, heat regulation, and so on. It has been calculated that the conscious mind can process about 126 bits of information per second, while the unconscious mind is processing about one million bits of information per second! We may say that most of our life is experienced at the unconscious level.

Additionally, the subconscious mind contains a "memory" of all that you have been or done, anything that has taken place in your experience from the moment of conception. These "memories" create beliefs, ideas, habits, and reflexes that cause a person to respond in life in certain ways. Sometimes these responses are beneficial and sometimes they are not. No one is born with a habit or a phobia; it is created over time by something that started it off. When wishing to "undo" the habit or phobia, one needs to discover what created it to begin with.

It is possible to take a journey into the subconscious mind, to explore its database and to make discoveries. It knows things that the conscious mind does not know, for example, why someone has an elevator phobia. It has the answers one needs for their healing. Often when accessing an unknown reason for something going on, the patient has an "aha" moment. This knowledge, in and of itself, can begin the healing process.

But how can we access this vast database residing within the subconscious mind? While the conscious mind works with logic, judgments, and decision-making, the subconscious mind works entirely differently. One can "talk" to it by creating pictures in the mind, known as imagery or visualization, and through stories and parables. In these ways, the hypnotist can access and activate responses in the subconscious mind, giving it suggestions for change, or guiding it to discover what needs to happen for healing. When the subconscious mind "trusts" that the hypnotherapist has positive intentions and is working for its ultimate benefit, it will go along with the suggestions being implanted.

The beginning of the hypnotic experience involves bringing the patient into a very relaxed and focused state, known as a trance. One is focused inward on his inner experience or on the voice of the hypnotherapist, and they disconnect from the outside world. In our daily lives, we often go in and out of trances spontaneously, for example, when driving on a straight and boring highway we can lose track of where we are or we pass our exit without realizing it. This is known as "highway hypnosis." Or, if you ever daydream while washing the dishes, you may suddenly look into the sink and wonder when the dirty dishes got washed.

And so, a trance state is not something foreign to us. The hypnotherapist knows how to use this state to access the patient's subconscious mind and then use various techniques to bring about mind-body healing. By utilizing the power within the subconscious mind, the healing can often occur easily and effortlessly. In other situations, the process might be more painful as old traumas are dealt with or when someone is in denial of certain aspects of his life and is awakened to his reality. But the beauty of the art of hypnosis is that the answers that lie within can be gently brought forth to bring about healing when, in some cases, that seemed an impossible dream.

1

IRRATIONAL FEARS

Leora Davis

Leora had multiple fears. She was afraid of the dark, afraid of being at home alone, afraid to walk outside alone once the sun had set, and, one might say, even afraid of her own shadow. At night, after putting the children to bed, once her husband left the house for night *seder* in his *kollel*, she locked the front door and went from room to room checking the closets and under the beds to be sure no one was there. Although she never found someone hiding in her closets, she nevertheless remained fearful until her husband came home later that night. She never even locked the bathroom door, afraid she might get locked inside, unable to get out.

She had several children and had to function as a wife and mother, but the stress of her fears and trying to keep them hidden from her children was debilitating. Her doctor had put her on anti-anxiety drugs, but they had not been very helpful. She decided that it was high time to get rid of her irrational fears and behaviors and begin living life normally.

I accepted Leora as a client only after I had verified that she knew her fears were imaginary and irrational. Had she expressed in any way that she actually believed someone was hiding in her home, although she could not find him, I would not have accepted her as a client. I would not treat people who were delusional or suffered from mental illness. That was outside the scope of my expertise.

Leora and her husband tended to downplay the severity of her symptoms, saying that she functioned quite well in daily life. Therefore, I decided I would try changing her behaviors without delving into the root cause. I had learned from experience that it was not always necessary to discover the cause of behaviors, as oftentimes the cause was long gone although the behavior remained in place as an ingrained habit. If I were successful in changing her current negative behaviors and reactions to situations, we would save ourselves many additional therapy sessions.

Hypnosis is an altered state of consciousness. Very simply said, this means that the client's brain waves have changed from causing her to be in a wide-awake alert state (Gamma and Beta waves) to being in a state in which she feels as though she is daydreaming (Alpha and Theta waves). This is not a sleep state (Delta waves) and during hypnosis she may hear sounds, such as the telephone ringing or a dog barking. She will experience them as very insignificant background sounds, or she simply may not hear them at all. This is what is meant by being in trance. When someone is in trance, what she imagines appears to her to be real, as though she is experiencing it in the moment or watching it on a movie screen. If the therapy is effective, the things she imagines may very well become her new reality.

It is not uncommon for us to go into a trance state without trying, such as when we spontaneously daydream or when driving on a very long, boring road and go into what is known as "highway hypnosis." In that state we lose awareness of our surroundings and may miss our exit without realizing what has happened.

When I work with a client, I put her into a trance by speaking very slowly, in a gentle and soothing way, like one might do when lulling a child to sleep. This is known as the hypnotic induction. She will feel disconnected from the outside world and is focused instead on my voice and on her internal experience. However, in a situation of danger, such as the smoke alarm going off, her internal mechanism that keeps her safe would immediately bring her out of the trance and give her the ability to get up and run out of the house. In a state of hypnosis, I cannot make a client do something she doesn't want to do because of her innate internal safety mechanism that is always working to protect her.

Putting Leora into hypnosis was not a simple task. Her hyper vigilance and fear of danger kept her out of trance for quite some time. But once she allowed me to induce a trance state, I prayed to Hashem that I would be able to work with her effectively. Although she was in a deep trance, she was able to hear me and answer my questions. Her speech was slow and took some effort to produce, a sign that she was in hypnosis.

"Leora," I asked, "is there someone in your present life or in your past whom you consider brave and fearless?"

She thought for a moment and then said, "Yes.... Sandy is one of my summer camp counselors."

"See yourself in camp now...with Sandy.... Nod your head to let me know when you are there."

She nodded.

"How old are you, Leora?"

"Fifteen."

"Just right.... What makes you think that Sandy is brave and fearless?" I wanted some more details about Sandy's personality.

"I know that she could do anything...she decided to do...no matter how hard.... I adore her!"

"Would she do you a favor?.... Would she help you out...if you asked her to?"

"Of course she would!.... She helps everyone...no matter how hard it is."

I could see that Sandy was a perfect model of courage and goodness in Leora's eyes, and perfect for our needs.

"Good.... Leora, I'd like you to see yourself standing alongside Sandy.... Tell me when you can see her next to you...or sense that you are standing next to her."

Since I cannot be sure that Leora will see Sandy in her mind's eye, I gave her the option of sensing her presence. I waited patiently for her to imagine her counselor standing right there with her.

"OK.... She's here."

"Now, Leora, ask Sandy if she would share...some of her courage with you...because you're missing some...and need it right now."

Leora's response was quick in coming. "I asked.... She said she would."

"Good!.... Very good! Now stand side by side with Sandy.... Stand a little closer to her...and closer....Very good!.... Now I'd like your right arm to touch her left arm...and move closer...and feel yourself moving into Sandy's body...until the two of you are slowly merging into one person.... Can you feel that?"

She nodded in the affirmative.

"Feel her bravery and fearlessness coursing through your body...and feel the energy of your newfound courage.... Can you feel that?.... Tell me when you feel that bravery and fearlessness...that courage...moving through your body...."

After a short pause she said, "Yes.... I can feel it.... It feels so good!"

"That's right!.... Very good!.... Now, see yourself acting as a courageous woman...in any way you wish.... You can hear Sandy whispering in your ears...telling you how brave you are...and how you know exactly what to do.... Let me know when you have done that."

I waited until she nodded. I then guided her through various visualizations in which she imagined herself acting fearlessly and resolutely. She was able to see herself save her children from harm, make wise decisions, strengthen her husband in his times of need, and more.

Before bringing Leora out of hypnosis, I had her separate out of Sandy's body as I did not want her to imagine she was Sandy; I wanted her to feel herself as an independent person, but with the addition of Sandy's positive qualities she had received.

This approach, of experiencing newly acquired courage, was successful to some degree but never completely eradicated Leora's fears. Although she did progress in some situations, there were others in which she reverted to her old fear patterns. I realized there must be something from her past that kept her in this hyper-alert mode, and I knew I had to look for the root cause, even if that meant taking her back to her distant childhood.

Under hypnosis, I discovered several incidents that created fear, ones that were unexpected and thrust upon her suddenly. She had not been able to defend herself or to escape from them since they had appeared without prior notice.

She told me of one incident when she, at the age of eight, had taken the bag of garbage from her house out to the large bin in the yard. It was just turning dark as she prepared to throw the bag in, when her three brothers jumped out from behind some bushes making frightening ghostlike sounds. Sure that they were devils, she dropped the garbage and ran, sobbing hysterically, into the house. Subsequently, her brothers took every opportunity to jump out from a hiding place, especially after dark, and scare her. It did not take long for her to become hyper-alert whenever the day waned or whenever she was in an unfamiliar place.

Each time something happened to scare her, the pattern of fearfulness was strengthened and reinforced. Over time, her grasp of reality became so distorted that a dark cat passing in front of her would send her into hysterics. Shadows became imaginary ghosts out to get her. Once the pattern was firmly ingrained, she no longer needed to see anything suspicious in order to feel fright. Her imagination provided the "devil," whether or not it was actually there.

Her father was another source of fear in her life. He often hit and punished her unjustly and she came to fear the nighttimes when he returned from work. He had wanted a son when she was born after two older sisters. His disappointment at having a girl made him act harshly toward her from as far back as she could remember. Once her brothers were born, he was so used to treating Leora as the black sheep of the family that the habit remained entrenched—despite the fact that he now had three sons as well as three daughters.

The incident that cut deeply into her heart and made her cry when telling me about it was when her father punished her severely for something her brother did. Even when he later found out the truth, he never apologized to his daughter for the injustice he had dealt her. Leora took this incident as a proof of her father's hatred for her. I knew Leora would need to do some forgiveness work before she could truly release the resentments of the past that were chaining her to her fears. Once she could forgive the people creating her fears and let go of the resentments she harbored, she would be empowered to release her paranoid behaviors resulting from those fears.

"Leora, are you aware that when we are angry at others and hold resentment in our hearts, we hurt ourselves more than those we are angry at?" I asked her at the beginning of our session.

"What do you mean 'we hurt ourselves'?" she wanted to know.

"Keeping anger and resentment inside ourselves is like storing acid in our bodies. The stress hormones those negative emotions produce, like adrenalin, cortisol, and norepinephrine in levels higher than normal, can cause a lot of damage over time. Sometimes, forgiving someone may feel like you are doing them a favor, but in truth, you are doing yourself a favor. When you can let go of old resentments you feel lighter and freer. Women have told me after a forgiveness session that it felt like a stone was rolling off their chest. And once that happens you can heal in so many ways. What do you think about doing that yourself?"

She sat silently, contemplating what I was saying. I think this was the first time she had been exposed to concepts such as these. I trusted that her innate intelligence would help her make the decision to go ahead.

After several minutes of thinking things over, she looked up at me. "What if my pain hurts so much that I can't forgive?" she wanted to know.

"If your pain hurts so much," I answered softly, "that is exactly the reason you would want to do this forgiveness work. Then your pain will just simply melt away."

"How is it possible?"

"The only way to know is to try it. If it won't work for you, it won't work. But you won't be worse off than before trying. But if it does work, you will begin to feel so much better."

She remained silent while I waited patiently for her to make her decision. I did not say a word about the mitzvah explicitly stated in the Torah of "*lo sitor*," of letting go of resentment, the prohibition of bearing a grudge. I did not want to pressure her into agreeing to do "forgiveness" therapy. I wanted her to *want* to do it.

The minutes stretched on in silence. I was beginning to to wonder if Leora was actually going to go ahead with this vital piece of therapy. I felt relieved when she finally spoke up. "OK. Let's do it."

"Good, Leora. I know you will be happy that you made this effort to forgive....

"Make yourself comfortable in the chair..." I began to intone. I took my time in putting her into a medium trance.

"Today we will go on a journey...a very special journey.... You will be safe and protected...as Hashem will accompany you on this special journey...this special mitzvah journey....For what can be better than letting go of hatred...anger...resentment?.... You will come out of this journey...cleansed...pure...*tahor*...as though you are a newborn infant.... Hashem wants you to succeed...and He will help you succeed...on this special journey."

I had her imagine herself going down a long road back into the past, as far back as she felt she needed to go. I then had her imagine a lovely little cottage, with a beautiful flower garden surrounding it. She let me know that she could hear the birds chirping and smell the fragrant flowers. I sensed that she was completely immersed in her surroundings. She could see the words I told her were written on the front door, "FORGIVENESS HUT." I told her to let the words engrave themselves into her brain.

"Now, Leora, go up to the door and let yourself in to the hut.... It has been waiting a long time for you to come.... It is so happy that you are finally here.... Can you feel the welcome it is giving you?"

I waited, unsure of her response, and rejoiced when she nodded in the affirmative.

"Make yourself at home.... Do whatever you need to do...to feel comfortable....Perhaps you'd like to say some *Tehillim*...or turn on some music...or eat something...whatever you want to do.... Take your time to enjoy this lovely place....Feel how much this place can help you...to succeed in achieving forgiveness...so that you can heal."

I maintained a lengthy pause, allowing her time to absorb the positive energy of her surroundings.

"And whenever you feel ready...please invite the first person you want to forgive...to join you here.... Take as much time with him or her as you need...until you know that forgiveness has taken place.... And then keep on inviting...one by one...all the other people...you want to do forgiveness with.... When you have finished...just let me know with a nod of your head."

I did not instruct her on how to accomplish the forgiveness. I trusted that her subconscious mind would know exactly what to do. Of course, I had primed her all along by saying what a great mitzvah she was doing, and that Hashem would surely help her to succeed. I felt fairly certain that her goal would be attained.

To begin with, I had felt apprehensive that Leora would show resistance in forgiving her tormentors. After all, she could rightfully blame them for the years of distress they had caused her. But I believed, that with *siyata d'Shmaya*, she could move along smoothly, going through the process successfully. Surprisingly, the task was accomplished much more easily than I ever imagined. I think Leora so desperately wanted a better quality of life that she was ready to do anything to improve things.

While in the "Forgiveness Hut," she went through separate sessions with her father, her mother who had done little to protect her, and with each of her three brothers. When she indicated to me that she was finished, I brought her out of hypnosis.

"How do you feel?" I asked

"So much better, I can't even believe it! It feels just like you said, like a stone rolled of my chest."

"I'm really glad to hear that! And besides feeling so much better, you also fulfilled a Torah commandment of not bearing a grudge, *lo sitor*. You can feel really proud of yourself for doing this!"

I knew how powerful the act of forgiveness was, how much this was the will of the *Borei Olam,* and believed her life would change dramatically as a result.

"Now the test is to see what you can do in real life," I continued. "I want you to think of some way that you can express this newfound forgiveness to someone in your life. Think about it and tell me when something comes to mind."

She struggled for a few minutes. Finally, she said, "I never invite my father to come over. Once in a while, he comes on his own to visit his grandchildren, and I treat him nicely. But I never ask him to come. I think," she said hesitantly, "that I'll invite him over for his birthday and have my mother, sisters, and brothers come, and we'll make him a party."

"That's amazing!" I exclaimed. "How soon is his birthday?"

"In about three weeks.... I'm sure I could not have done this before our session. I'm still not sure I'll have the courage...."

"Stop!" I immediately interrupted. "Don't even let that thought enter your mind. Of course, you'll have the courage to do it! Sandy will be whispering in your ears and giving you some of her courage! You are not the same person you were before today. You are the new, courageous, fearless Leora! Think of yourself that way and you will be that way."

I continued encouraging her and could see that my words were penetrating. Her expression changed slowly to one of enthusiasm and confidence. I was sure she would do well. She later reported that the party she made was a huge success, and this was something that had seemed to her far beyond her capabilities.

Subsequently, Leora let me know that she had actually spoken to her father about that hurtful incident of the past, when she was punished unjustly. She let him know how much it had affected her, but nevertheless still wanted a real and caring relationship with him. He was very moved by her openness, expressed his sorrow, and actually asked for her forgiveness. She'd never imagined in her wildest dreams that this could happen, but it had. Her new relationship with her father gave her validation as a person in her own right, and allowed her to feel herself a vital, capable human being. Her fears melted away, almost effortlessly, and she became, as one might say, a new person.

I once again saw how amazing hypnotherapy can be for creating positive change.

2

PHOBIAS

Marla Goodman

Marla suffered from an imaginary feeling of falling. Whenever she missed a step, stumbled, or was startled, she was sure she was falling into a deep abyss. Her heart would pound and she'd often feel dizzy. It would take her a good few minutes to get her bearings and her stability back. Sometimes she'd remain shaky for the rest of the day.

Under hypnosis, I took her back in time to try to discover the source of this imaginary feeling. It was an interesting journey.

Once I put her into trance, I had her imagine a long road in front of her.

I intoned slowly, "See yourself standing on this road, this long, long road.... The signpost reads 'Back in Time'.... See yourself now walking down the road back in time...back in time...back in time...back in time...back to a time in your life...when you had an issue with falling.... When you get there just let me know...."

I then remained silent, waiting for her response.

Marla's first response came rather quickly. She spoke slowly, with difficulty, a good sign that she was deep in trance.

"It's raining...it's dark outside.... It's hard to see where I'm going.... I just bumped into something.... I'm falling, falling flat on my face.... I'm crying...."

"When did this happen? How old are you?" I asked.

"I'm pregnant with my second baby.... I'm twenty-eight...."

"Is someone helping you up?" I always address the person in trance in the present tense, as they relive the memory as though it were taking place at that moment.

"Two ladies are working so hard...to pull me up.... They want to take me to the hospital.... I don't want to go.... I hate hospitals.... I say I'm fine...."

"That's right.... You are fine.... There are always people ready to help you up.... No one will ever leave you lying on the ground.... Now you can go home and rest...."

She nodded.

"When you fell this time...was the feeling new to you...or was it familiar?"

"Familiar."

"That's right...familiar.... Let us go back in time...to an earlier time when you fell or thought you were falling...."

I repeated the suggestions again and again of her going back in time to an earlier incident involving falling. At some point, she answered my question about the feeling as "new," which indicated we had reached the first time it had happened. That incident is called "the initial sensitizing event"—ISE for short. It is most important that we discover what that first trigger was. The events that follow are less important to deal with than the ISE. That one is what began creating a pattern in her mind, and each subsequent event solidified the pattern until a full-blown phobia was created.

Now my job was to revisit each event and help her reframe it in her mind so that the fear and helplessness would be neutralized. Subsequently, she would be able to remember each event, but the fear, the despair, and the distress would no longer accompany the memory. The memories would become passive after losing their emotional charge, and would no longer trigger negative feelings. Once the memories were rendered harmless, any incident involving falling or something reminding her of falling would no longer have the ability to trigger negative feelings. The pattern that had been built up over years would now, in effect, no longer exist. The hope was that she now would respond to falling as any other person would.

Marla had reexperienced five separate incidents related to falling, some of them no longer consciously remembered. I had to effectively neutralize the fear, pain, or embarrassment she felt at that time in order to disempower the memory.

To do so, I wanted her to realize that there was a wise woman within her who knew how to act with integrity and love. I, therefore, elicited from her several incidences in which she had helped her children or others with loving-kindness and wisdom, through intelligent decision-making. I would use this "wise woman" aspect of herself as a resource in our healing process.

The incidents involving falling that Marla had uncovered went chronologically back in time. The event before falling in pregnancy was when, as a young newlywed, she fell from the ladder while hanging the sukkah decorations. The one before that happened as a high school teen being pushed by a rival in the ice-skating rink. Her ungraceful fall had made her the laughingstock of her classmates. Prior to that, the school bully had pushed her off the slide in the school playground and the injury she suffered required a few stitches. It seemed that the initial sensitizing event had occurred when, as an eight-month-old baby exploring her home on all fours, she fell down a flight of stairs and suffered a concussion. She had actually learned of this incident from her mother and reexperienced it now while in trance.

I put her into a fairly deep trance and called forth the wise woman within. I dubbed her "Wise Mrs. Goodman." I spoke directly to that part of Marla, as though she were an individual separate from the other aspects of Marla.

"Thank you, Wise Mrs. Goodman…for appearing today…. I'm sure you realize that Marla, young Marla, and baby Marla are hurting…. Would you be willing to help them heal from their pain and embarrassment? ….Would you be willing to help them get rid of their fear of falling?"

After a moment, I asked Marla, "What did Wise Mrs. Goodman say?"

"She's willing to help."

"Excellent! Let us begin the journey back in time…. Marla, bring Wise Mrs. Goodman…to the time you were twenty-eight years old and fell down…when you were pregnant…. Let me know when you are there."

When Marla indicated that they had arrived, I said, "Wise Mrs. Goodman, please comfort pregnant Marla…who is crying after her fall…. Please do your best to make her feel better…."

I waited while the scene was unfolding in Marla's mind. After an appropriate pause I spoke directly to the younger Marla. "Pregnant Marla, are you feeling better now?"

"Yes."

"What did Wise Mrs. Goodman tell you?"

"She hugged me…sat with me on the bench…and said that I will be fine…and my baby is fine…unhurt…. In a day or two…my bruises will be all healed…. She told me I am careful…not negligent…. It's not my fault…. Everyone falls sometimes…. It happens to us all…. Nothing to be afraid of…."

"And how do you feel now?" I asked her.

"Good…like I did before I fell down."

"That's right…. Thank Wise Mrs. Goodman for her kind words…. Stay well and healthy."

We left her and moved on. We visited each event, from the most recent to the older ones chronologically back in time. In each situation, I had the Wise Mrs. Goodman help, comfort, use first aid, love, and nurture the younger one in the most appropriate way for that scenario. By the time we were finished, the baby was happy and babbling away on Wise Mrs. Goodman's lap, completely at peace with her world.

Although we hadn't rewritten history, hadn't recreated what had actually happened, we had successfully revised how Marla was now perceiving and relating to those incidents. They were no longer terrifying and threatening to reoccur again and again in her life, as though falling was inevitable and to be her sorry fate for the rest of her life. Once the younger selves (including her adult younger selves) felt loved and cared for at this deepest level, she could trust that the world was a safe place. The proof of this was that her irrational panic attacks were no longer triggered.

Marla called me excitedly only a few days after our latest session.

"Bracha! You won't believe this! I was running after the kids in the playground and tripped. I caught myself from falling in time and waited for the panicky feelings to overwhelm me, as they always had in the past. But they never came. I sat down on a bench to make sure. And there I was, just like anyone else, taking a near fall as a normal part of life. I'm so excited!"

"I surely do believe it, Marla. Your phenomenal mind did this! You really don't have to come back anymore. Consider yourself healed."

"Thank you! Thank you, Bracha! I can't believe it! But I do believe it, because I experienced the change in myself just like that; completely and naturally—just by itself."

"Remember, though, you did the work. You spent the time, effort, and money to attain healing. And Hashem gave you the ability to do it."

3

OBSESSIVE THINKING

Rochel Miller

Rochel was a sweet young woman, who had grown up in a Chassidic community in New York. I met her on one of my trips to London, where she had moved after her marriage. She appeared tense when she came for her first session.

As always, I try to put my clients at ease before I begin with the questions that give me the background information needed for doing therapy. I usually start with small talk.

"Have a seat, Rochel, and make yourself comfortable. Would you like some water?"

"No thanks," she replied. "I had a drink before I came."

"I'm enjoying the cool weather here. It can be really hot in May in Eretz Yisrael."

"Yes, I enjoy it too," she said, somewhat stiffly.

"You sound American. Are you?"

She nodded in the affirmative.

"Have you been here long?"

"For the past five years, since I got married. I'm from Brooklyn, but my husband's from here."

"Do you like living in London?" I asked, fully focusing my gaze on her. I wanted her to feel that I was really interested in what she had to say.

"Quite. The people are nice and the children are happy. My husband's parents are warm and kind and make me feel a part of their family." She spoke quietly, controlled, without conveying emotion.

"So, what brings you here today?"

She looked down at her hands and clenched her teeth. Then she let out a deep sigh and lifted her gaze to me. "I have these thoughts, disturbing thoughts. I can't get rid of them." Her voice was still restrained.

"Please tell me about them," I said with empathy.

"They don't make any sense. I know they're not true, but they keep coming back...."

She became silent and I waited patiently for her to continue.

She suddenly spat out the words, much louder than before. "One thought says that I don't believe in Hashem. What kind of crazy thought is that? Of course I believe in Hashem! Another thought says that Hashem hates me and is out to get me! And there are other ones I'm too ashamed to talk about!"

She was becoming more agitated with each passing moment.

"Rochel," I said gently. "Take a deep breath and let it out slowly.... Continue taking those nice, long, deep breaths," I said.

She followed my instructions, and I could see her calming down.

"That's right, you're doing fine."

I let her take about ten breaths before I continued to speak.

"Any time you feel upset or anxious, stop and take some deep breaths. OK?"

She shook her head.

"Do you ever have thoughts of harming yourself?"

I had to know if she was feeling suicidal. In that case, I would have to refer her on to the appropriate professionals.

"No, of course not! I just feel so ashamed for having these ridiculous thoughts, but I can't get them to stop."

"How often do you have them?"

"When I'm busy, like teaching or taking care of the children, I don't have time to think. But when it's quiet and I'm with myself, they're always there."

"What happens to you as a result of these thoughts?" I wanted to know if they were affecting her life in any substantial way.

"I'm nervous, anxious, I shout, I get headaches, I'm super-sensitive to criticism and sometimes I can't fall asleep. My husband wonders what happened to me, but I can't tell him. He'll think I'm an *apikores* or gone crazy!"

"Does he know you came here today?"

"Yes. I told him I wanted help with my anxiety, and he was in complete agreement with me that I needed to get help. Do you think you can help me?" She sounded more than a little desperate.

"I've dealt numerous times with obsessive thinking and have achieved good results. If you are willing to practice the exercises I give you, I'm confident that with Hashem's help, you can get those results too."

My tone of voice conveyed the confidence I wanted her to feel. If she felt confident in my ability to help her, she would also feel confident in her ability to attain the goals we set out to achieve. Her response was less than ideal.

"I don't know if I'll be able to. That voice in my head is so scary. It makes me feel weak."

The tears that suddenly appeared threatened to spill over. I handed her a tissue. I waited until she finished wiping her eyes. She seemed embarrassed at her show of emotion.

"It's all right, Rochel," I said encouragingly. "You can allow yourself to express what you're feeling here. It's good to let it out once in a while. You know, the effort you put into covering up your upset can give you a headache, or it can make you so tense that you can't fall asleep at night. So in my office you can let out your emotions without hesitation. But at the same time, I'll teach you how not to be scared of that voice in your head. And then gradually, over time, you'll hear the voice without becoming upset. And, before you know it, the voice will go away. Would you like that?"

"Of course I'd like that. But it can't be that simple!" she looked in utter disbelief.

"If you follow the instructions I will give you and use the tools I'll teach you, it is that simple. But I don't know how long it will take. For some people, it's a short process, and for others it may be much longer. Since I'm staying in London for only a few weeks, you'll continue doing what I teach you on your own for as long as it takes to achieve the results you want. And, if necessary, from time to time, we'll have a session by phone. But I assure you, these techniques work."

"I'll try," she said quietly.

"No, Rochel, you won't try!" I said very firmly. "You will, *b'siyata d'Shmaya*, do whatever you learn here. You will not try, because 'try' means that you might fail. I want you to decide right now that you will do all the exercises every day, barring an emergency. I don't want to hear you say, 'I'll try' or 'I hope' or 'maybe.' And completely eliminate 'I can't'. From now on you will say, '*B'ezras Hashem*, I will' or 'I am' or 'I can.' These words express your belief that you will succeed, and they will make a tremendous difference. They will influence your behavior. Does this make sense?"

She nodded her head in the affirmative but didn't look convinced.

"What if I really can't do something or don't know how? What should I say then?" she questioned.

"You simply say, 'I couldn't do it till now' or 'I didn't know what to do till now. But now I'm learning how to do it.' You leave yourself open to the possibility of change. Does that sound reasonable?"

"Yes, I guess so."

"Good. I want you to say out loud what you have now decided." I made sure that while my tone was firm, my facial expression was kindly and full of caring.

She took a few moments to collect her thoughts. "*B'ezras Hashem*, I will do all the exercises Mrs. Toporowitch gives me, every day, for as long as I need to. If I have any questions or doubts, I will speak to her about them." Her tone, full of conviction, conveyed to me that she meant exactly what she was saying.

A huge smile broke out across my face. "Excellent! Beautiful! You got it just right! I'm really proud of you!" I was not exaggerating. I was really encouraged that she had gotten the message.

Rochel looked relieved, happy, and confident all at the same time.

"OK. I think the time has come to get started," I said looking at my watch. "Would you like that?"

"Yes, I can't wait. I'm glad we set up a double session for today. I see we really could use the extra time."

"Do you have any questions about hypnosis?" I asked.

"I sort of know what it is," she replied. "You talk to my subconscious mind and tell it what to do."

Her simplistic description of hypnosis caused me to smile. "Well, yes and no. I do talk to your subconscious mind, but I can't tell it what to do. It has to agree with the suggestions that I wish to implant. Your subconscious mind is always looking to protect you and if I give it a suggestion that it is opposed to, it will reject it. If it believes that the advice I am suggesting is to your advantage and ultimate benefit, it will accept it. So part of my job is enabling the subconscious mind to understand that I am working for you, trying to help you, and that what I am suggesting it does will only benefit you in the end. When that happens, your subconscious mind will embrace the suggestion I am offering and use it to bring about the changes we wish to achieve.

"Also, when talking to the subconscious mind, we don't have to use logic, as we do when addressing the conscious mind. Once it realizes I am working for you, it will accept any suggestion I give it, no matter how implausible it sounds. "

She nodded in understanding.

"The first thing I want you to know is that the voice in your head has no power to cause you to do anything or to harm you in any way, unless you let it. Let me repeat that in another way. The only power it has is what you give it.

"I'll explain what I mean. Take, for example, a little cockroach. Who is stronger, you or it? If you approach it, it runs for its life. It knows that with your one well-placed step its life is over. However, many women run from the cockroach in fear, as though it could do them harm. The fear they feel is self-induced, for the cockroach has no power to hurt those women in any way. However, because of this self-induced fear, the woman's heart may be racing, she may break out in a sweat, and so on. This is the power she has given to the lowly cockroach. If she'd had no fear she would not have been affected in that way.

"Now, I'm not saying that everything we are afraid of is powerless to harm us. I wouldn't say that about a black widow spider, for example. That spider is poisonous and should be feared. I'm talking about having fear of something that is powerless to do you harm. And that includes the thoughts you have. Do you know what a thought is?"

She shook her head in the negative.

"It's just a bit of electric current moving through your brain's neurons and synapses. More accurately, it's an electrochemical reaction. Whether it creates a reaction in your body is almost always up to you."

She looked at me wide-eyed, rather bewildered.

"But those thoughts are stronger than I am! I can't control them, no matter how much I try!" Rochel's voice was shaking with emotion.

"Let me rephrase that statement for you, if I may. 'But those thoughts *seem* to be stronger that I am. *Until now* I have not been able to control them, no matter how much I tried. I'm looking forward to learning how to do that.'

"How does saying it that way make you feel?" I looked at her expectantly.

After a moment of reflection, she smiled at me. "It certainly sounds much better. It gives me a feeling that I'm not stuck in a hopeless situation."

"You certainly are not. As soon as you start practicing the techniques I give you, you'll be on your way to controlling those thoughts.

"The first thing you do is learn to rephrase your negative thoughts and statements into ones that are either neutral or positive. Our negative thoughts and words affect us negatively, and our positive thoughts and words affect us positively. This is a skill we all have to learn."

"Can you give me an example?" she asked.

"Sure. Let's say it starts raining. You say, 'Uch, it's raining and I don't have an umbrella. I'm going to get drenched!' You are quite annoyed and your brain produces chemicals, called stress hormones, which make you feel tense, angry, and even feel pain. They might make you snap at your children or husband when you get home. So in order for this situation—rain that will cause you to get wet—to not affect you negatively, you need to express yourself differently. For example, 'Oh, it's raining. Great! I'm glad I won't have to water my lawn and my rose bushes today.' You're simply looking at what's happening in a different way that can actually be beneficial to you. In that state of mind, your brain will be producing what we call 'the happy hormones.' And then you will feel more positive, which will result in you behaving in a more positive way."

"Are you saying that even though I'll come home all wet, I won't feel irritable and won't snap at the children?" she asked incredulously.

"Yes, if you've done the positive thinking first. It's because your brain will be producing different brain chemicals in response to your thoughts and feelings."

"Wow! That's amazing!"

"Rochel, I'm going to give you some homework to do. Here's a list of sentences that I've written down. They are all of a negative nature. I want you to reframe each one so that they are either neutral or positive, just as we did now. Bring the completed sheet with you to our next session. If you get used to doing this, you will immediately see the results in your daily life."

I handed her a sheet of paper, an assignment I give to many of my clients.

"This is just the foundation of our work on your obsessive thinking. The first step is for you to realize that you have a certain amount of control over your thoughts. You may not have control when the thought first pops into your head. But you do have control over what you do with it afterward. Do you let it overpower you or do you show it that you are the boss and you can decide what to do with it?"

"OK," she responded. "I'm ready to do anything to give me control over my horrid thoughts! But what makes them come?"

Normally, I would want to uncover the reason for her obsessive thoughts. However, in this situation, since my trip to England was nearly over, I feared that I did not have enough time to search for and work with the root cause. In numerous situations I find it is possible to work with the symptoms only, no matter what is bothering the client, and resolve the issue this way. If the strategy I proposed to use with Rochel worked, we would accomplish the goal in the short amount of time remaining for my visit. If the strategy did not work, I would then need to delve deeper into discovering the reason for her obsessive thinking and work with her on those issues in a subsequent visit to England or by telephone. For now, I would try to alleviate the problem by working on the negative thoughts alone.

"I don't know at this point. But it might not even be important to know why. If we can correct the problem by doing the exercises, we really don't need to know the reason for them. If you practice what I teach you, I'm quite convinced you will be free of them."

She smiled and her shoulders dropped ever so slightly, a clear sign of tension being released.

"Are you ready for some hypnosis?" I asked.

"Sure!"

"Make yourself comfortable in the chair." I spoke slowly using what I called my "hypno-voice."

"Allow your head to be supported by the back of the chair...and focus on your breathing...."

I used a slow hypnotic induction, nudging her gently into relaxation. When I saw signs of hypnosis, I used testing to gauge how deep the trance was and continued inducing deeper and deeper states. At the point when she was unable to open her eyes, raise her arm off the armrest, or lower her arm after I lifted it into the air, I felt ready to begin therapy.

"Rochel, notice how good you feel in this relaxed state.... You feel strong and confident.... Strong and confident.... You know that you are stronger, much stronger than you were just a short while ago...."

I let the message sink into her subconscious mind for several moments.

"You are now at home...strong and confident...and it is quiet...and you have nothing much to do....

"There is a knock at the door.... You look through the peephole and see a dirty, smelly, deranged woman...yelling and screaming.... You know this woman...she transmits contagious diseases.... When she comes, you can't get rid of her.... She sits around for hours...scaring the children out of their wits.... The poor kids can't fall asleep on the nights after her visits.... You are very upset.... You don't want to let her into the house because you know the children will be petrified...and she is a danger to you and the family.... But she keeps on knocking.... What should you do?....

"If you open the door, she will get in...and you won't be able to get rid of her.... If you tell her, 'Go away,' she will know you are home and will continue knocking.... She is very persistent.... If you stay quiet she will not know you are home...and after knocking for a while with no response, she will leave.... She knows there is no point in knocking...when no one is home....

"You let her knock without saying anything.... You are not afraid of her...she can't get into the house...the door is locked.... You see her through the peephole and you don't care.... It doesn't bother you.... You know she will go away soon...because she cannot get in.... If you don't react...she will go away.... You are not afraid of her...because she can't open the door...and she will leave soon.... You look at her through the peephole...without emotion.... She cannot affect you....

The door is between you and her...and she doesn't know you are home...because you don't respond...and soon she will leave...."

Repetition is important in hypnosis as it embeds the suggestion firmly into the subconscious mind. I spent some time rephrasing the idea differently, using words and metaphors.

"When she goes away, you feel very good.... She did not get in...because you did not let her in.... You knew what to do...to be quiet and not react.... You did not feel afraid or upset...because you knew what to do...and she went away....

"She has a right to exist...because Hashem created her...and you have the right to let her in...or not to let her in....If you want, you can let her in...but if you don't want, you don't let her in....You look at her through the peephole...and you feel strong and confident...and relaxed...."

I waited a full minute in silence before continuing.

"Sometimes there are other things that want to get in...that you wish to keep out.... You know how to keep things or people out.... If there was a cockroach...on the other side of the door...you would know how to keep it out.... If there was a dragon...on the other side of the door...you would know how to keep it out.... If there was a thought you didn't like on the other side of the door...you would know how to keep it out.... You would feel strong and confident...and keep the door closed without saying anything...without reacting.... You would feel no emotion...because a thought has a right to exist...just as a cockroach has a right to exist...just as a deranged woman has a right to exist...but you don't have to let it in.... You have the right...and the ability to keep it out."

Again, I remained silent for several moments, allowing the message to sink in.

"Sometimes you are in a place when the thought comes...without a door between you and it...to keep it out.... So then, you place a strong glass wall...between you and it.... You can see through the glass...but someone on the other side cannot see you.... You can see the thought...you can observe it...but it doesn't bother you...because that strong glass wall is there...between you and it.... The thought cannot penetrate the glass wall.... That wall is very, very strong.... Nothing can penetrate that glass wall...it is so strong...unless you open the door in it.... And you have the control...and the confidence...to keep that door closed...when you wish...or open it when you wish....

"Wherever you are, whenever you need to...you can place that strong glass wall between you...and anything else you don't want to bother you.... All you have to do...is say, 'Hashem, please send me the glass wall now'...and it will be there instantly...because Hashem wants to help you...and protect you.... It is so simple...so easy.... You can do this so easily....

"Right now, you are going to do this...to bring the glass wall between you and something.... Because you know all you have to do is say...'Hashem, please send me the glass wall now'.... And it will be there instantly....

"Now, you can see in the distance a thought coming close.... It is a thought you don't like...and you don't want it to get into your head.... Maybe it looks like a deranged woman...maybe it looks like a cockroach...or a monster.... Whichever way you see it...you see it coming close.... You are strong and confident...you are not afraid.... Say now, to yourself...what you need to say to bring the strong glass wall...between you and the thought."

I paused, giving her the time to think the words.

"Let me know with a nod of your head...when the wall is there...in front of you."

I didn't question whether or not the wall would be there. My implication was that it would be there and so, in her mind, she was sure it would appear. After a moment, she nodded.

"Good, very good.... It is so simple to bring that wall there.... Now you know the thought cannot get to you.... It will be there on the other side of the wall...until it goes away.... But you don't care.... It can be there as long as it wants...because in the end it goes away...just like the deranged woman goes away...when you don't react....

"That was very easy for you, was it not?"

She nodded.

"You feel very safe and strong and confident, do you not?"

She nodded again.

"Now I'll teach you a trick...to make that wall come...with lightning speed...even if you don't have time to say...or think the words.... Would you like that, Rochel?

She nodded again.

"Once again the thought will approach...but this time when you say the words...'Hashem, please send me the glass wall now'...at the same time you press...the thumb and forefinger of your right hand together to form a circle.... Whenever you say those words...asking for the strong glass wall...you press the thumb and forefinger together.... Let's do it now."

I put her through the process five separate times and then made her do it on her own another five times.

"You have power in your fingers, Rochel.... You can bring the glass wall that will protect you...just by pressing your fingers together as you say the words.... Then one day, you won't even have to say the words.... You just press your fingers together...and the wall is there...."

I explained that her pressing her fingers together in that way while saying or thinking something is called an "anchor." An anchor becomes associated in a person's mind with his words or thoughts until they become firmly attached like a ship's anchor to the seabed. At that point the anchor is interchangeable with the words and is able to do what the words do. I explained the importance of repeating this exercise many times daily until the anchor can do what the words do. Then the glass wall would appear instantly just by pressing her fingers together.

"And now you no longer feel upset when the thoughts come...because they can't get into your head...because you know how to bring the wall instantly...by using your anchor.... Let's do it one more time...."

I put her through a scenario of her going to bed, fearful that she would be unable to fall asleep, as had happened to her so often in the past. I had her say the words and activate her anchor and feel the feelings of being safe and protected. Then I had her experience herself falling into a deep and peaceful sleep. Shortly after, I brought her slowly out of hypnosis. She opened her eyes and stretched.

"How do you feel?" I asked.

"That was amazing! Absolutely amazing! I literally felt that the glass wall was there, and I could see the thoughts on the other side. They looked like little ants crawling around. And I had no fear at all!"

"Wonderful! Your homework is to continue to practice activating your anchor many times a day while asking Hashem to send you the glass wall, as an exercise. Also, whenever you feel an unwanted thought approaching, you do the same. You do this exercise as soon as you realize a thought is coming and before it starts bothering you. The more you do it, the more effective it will be. And sometimes this technique won't work for you. So, on occasion when the thought gets into your head before you can stop it, I want you to know that it's OK. You can't perfect a skill in a day. But day by day, you will get better and better results. After all, some success is better than none. True?"

"Of course!"

"What percent of success during this coming week will make you happy?"

"Um, maybe 50 percent. But how long do you think it will take until I succeed every time at stopping the thoughts?"

"It doesn't really matter if you don't stop the thoughts. I want you to be able to have the thoughts and not be upset by them. It would be like watching ants crawling around on the ground and you couldn't care less.

"The negative thoughts are actually a tool of the *yetzer hara* to get you down and interfere with your *avodas Hashem*. Once the *yetzer hara* realizes that the thoughts aren't bothering you anymore and are not affecting your *avodas Hashem*, it becomes useless to keep sending them. They'll stop coming on their own without you having to do anything. It's like the deranged lady who will stop knocking on the door and go away after a while because no one is answering."

"Wow, I never thought of it that way, but it makes sense that it's the *yetzer hara* doing this to me. And since we now know its tactics we can, *b'siyata d'Shmaya*, win the battle!"

The glow on Rochel's face clearly expressed that she was having an "aha" moment. But I didn't want her to be disappointed because of unrealistic expectations.

"Rochel, remember what I said to begin with," I interjected quickly. "Some people go through the changes they are trying to achieve faster than others. So expect that it may take time. We never know. It will depend a lot upon how much you reframe your negative thinking in general and how often you practice activating your anchor.

"I'm going to give you one more bit of homework and that is to repeat an affirmation several times a day. An affirmation is a positive sentence and the more you say it, the more it changes your way of thinking and feeling. An example might be, 'I do not fear my negative thoughts and I am stronger than they are.' How does that sound?"

"Maybe something more like, 'My thoughts are powerless and I control them.'"

"Let's be more specific to what's going on here," I added. "After all, some thoughts are very powerful like 'Hashem loves and protects me.' How about, 'My *yetzer hara* thoughts are meaningless and do not affect me.' And even though they still are affecting you today, your affirmation is expressing a goal you are striving to achieve. You're stating that you are now on the path that is leading you there. Also, by saying your affirmation in the present tense, you're expressing that this goal has already started happening, day by day, little by little, more and more. Do you like that affirmation?"

"Yes. I think it's just right. When should I say it, and how often?"

"Say it whenever you remember, the more often the better. The best times are when you wake up, right after *modeh ani*, and before falling asleep. The morning affirmation will start your day off right and the one before sleep will remain with you all night. The best way to do it is by imagining yourself unaffected by the thoughts as you say the words."

I took out an index card and a black marker and told her to write the affirmation on it. I suggested that she make several cards and put them in places she would see them to act as reminders.

"Do you have any questions, Rochel, about what we did today?" I asked.

"No, everything is very clear."

I reviewed the several tasks I had given her and scheduled her for a session the following week. She left in a brighter mood than the one she had come in with.

Rochel was a good student and, although she said she'd be happy with a 50 percent success rate, she actually achieved at least 70 percent. We had another two sessions, by which time she was hardly ever bothered by the troublesome thoughts. And she knew that if they did come to visit from time to time, they would simply not affect her—as she knew exactly what to do with them.

I received a letter from her about a month after I got home. She told me that her life was totally changed, and she felt like a new person. She added that she was even using this technique to help some of her students. That is a heartwarming example of the ripple effect!

4

POST-TRAUMA AFFECTING
THE PRESENT

Aliza Sherman

I traveled regularly to London from Israel to work with the religious women in Stamford Hill. The Chassidic women in particular were averse to going to male practitioners, and I had plenty of clientele whenever I came.

It was on one of my longer stays that I met Aliza. She was a middle-aged woman who had by then married off most of her children. She had a twenty-eight-year-old son and a sixteen-year-old daughter still living at home.

As she sat opposite me in my clinic, she fidgeted nervously. I greeted her warmly with a big smile and then commented on the lovely sweater she was wearing. She thanked me for the compliment and relaxed visibly.

It was important to get the clients to relax before jumping in to the issue at hand.

"Please Aliza, please tell me what brings you here today."

I always avoided using the word "problem" or asking what was wrong. This was a technique of downplaying the severity of whatever was troubling her. In this open-ended way, we began our session.

"In general, I have a good relationship with my children. But with Shimon, my twenty-eight-year-old son, I have problems. He's very closed and won't share his feelings with me or even with my husband."

"How does he spend his day?" I wanted to know.

"He learns half a day and works afterward. When he comes home at night, he eats dinner, reads something, or calls a friend and goes to bed. I can never get into a real conversation with him. I feel he must have some kind of block stopping him from getting married because most of the *shidduchim* he goes on end pretty quickly. I can't help him in any way if he won't talk to me."

"It must be frustrating," I empathized with her, "to feel so stymied in your ability to help him."

"I would do anything to help him," she whispered, as the tears glistened in her eyes. "He went out with the last girl for half a year. We were sure he'd get engaged to her. Then it ended, just like that! He got cold feet and just couldn't commit."

It sounded to me that Shimon was the one who needed therapy. But Aliza had come to me and I had to try to find some way of helping her.

"Tell me, Aliza, in which way can I be of assistance to you?"

"I'm very tense about the situation and I'm not sleeping well. I sometimes get snappy. Shimon acts irritated when I talk to him. I must be transferring my stress to him."

"It seems so," I agreed with her, "and that's something we can deal with. I'll teach you several stress-management techniques to help you feel better. They will also enable you to communicate more easily with Shimon. You want him to feel that you are more laid-back about the situation, without expectations of him. It would be good if you could get him to believe that you are OK with him just the way he is."

"That makes sense. How do I do that?"

"I'll teach you several relaxation techniques that you will be able to do on your own at home. This will give you immediate relief. But beyond that, I'd like to explore Shimon's history a bit. Maybe we can discover what's causing him to be so closed, so noncommunicative. Perhaps something happened in the past that we need to pay attention to. Was he always so closed with you?"

Aliza shut her eyes and pondered my question. After a short while, she opened them and let out a sigh.

"For a really long time, way before his bar mitzvah, he's been like this. But I do remember him as a very young child, lively and talkative. He loved nursery school and played with the children. I even recall one of his teachers telling me that he was an ideal little boy, playing, interacting with the other children, picking up his toys when told to. Everything a preschool teacher could wish for!"

Aliza's description of little Shimon, portraying a person vastly different from the present one, set off a red flashing light in my mind. It seemed to indicate that the young Shimon had undergone some trauma that had completely altered his personality and his relationship with people. I had no way of knowing if Aliza held the key to unlocking the puzzle. She might have been completely unaware of what had happened to her child to shock his nervous system in such a profound way.

My plan was to begin therapy with stress management. The immediate need was for Aliza to learn to de-excite her nervous system when interacting with Shimon. Once she was more emotionally stable and able to self-soothe, I would attempt to discover what was at the root of Shimon's personality change.

I spent two sessions teaching Aliza breathing exercises and various techniques for relieving emotional pain and stress. She reported that she was sleeping better at night and had even had several short but meaningful conversations with Shimon. During this time, he had begun dating a girl and things were looking hopeful. I felt we were ready for the next phase of our therapy.

Aliza came to our third meeting in a good mood. I told her my plan for our session.

"I believe that now is a good time to try to discover that 'something' that might have caused Shimon to change so dramatically in his relationship with others. Do you feel ready to do that?"

She looked at me with questioning eyes that clearly expressed a bit of fear. She might have been afraid of discovering something that could point a finger of blame at her.

"I don't know.... I'm not sure...," was her hesitant reply.

"Aliza, there's nothing to be afraid of. Your subconscious mind will either give us the information or not. And it is equally possible that you do not have this information to share with me. But if you do, your subconscious mind will make the decision to bring it up if it is in your best interest to do so. In other words, if it is for your ultimate benefit to reveal to us what happened in the past to Shimon, it will do so."

She appeared relieved. "OK. Sure. Let's try."

I always want the client to feel in control of the situation and never, *chas v'shalom*, feel that I am making them do something against their will.

"Good!" I said emphatically. "You will most likely be very happy that we went down this road. In case you have no idea of what happened to create this change in Shimon, you will be freed of any guilt feelings you may be harboring. You will know that this has nothing to do with neglect or mistreatment on your part."

Aliza visibly relaxed and made herself comfortable in the chair. She responded well to my hypnotic cues, as we had worked successfully in our previous sessions. She went into a deep trance state easily and smoothly. I tested to ascertain how deep her trance was and then began the actual therapeutic work.

I had her imagine a large building in front of her with the word "LIBRARY" written in big bold letters above the entrance.

"Aliza, you are now entering the library. It contains records of all the memories of all the people in your life. That's why it is such a huge building. As you walk through it you will notice row upon row of books. Each row has a name attached to it. Your subconscious mind is now leading you to the row that has the name 'Aliza Sherman' written upon it. Let me know with a nod of your head when you have found the row of books bearing your name."

I remained quiet while she roamed through the vast area in her mind. Within a minute or two she nodded her head.

"Good! Very good! Now walk down the length of this row slowly...scanning all the books on the shelves.... Each book contains a different memory from your life.... All of your memories...from the moment you were created until the present...are recorded here....

"As you walk along this row, you will get the urge to stop somewhere.... You will stop near a book...that contains a memory...that is important for you to remember at this time.... It is a memory involving Shimon...and it has a bearing on his present difficulties.... If this memory is found here, it will call to you...and you will be drawn to it....

"As you walk slowly down the length of the row...pay attention to your feelings...to the messages you may be receiving.... You may feel like stopping next to a book...that seems important to you.... Let me know with a nod of your head when you stop."

I waited patiently. After a few minutes she nodded her head.

"Good! Very good!.... You are now standing next to the book...containing the memory we wish to examine.... Your hand is being drawn to that book.... You will feel an urge...to remove it from the shelf.... Let me know with a nod of your head...when you are holding that book."

This time her response came fairly quickly.

"Good! Very good!.... Take the book to a quiet corner of the reading room...find a seat and open the book.... You will read the story within.... Let me know when you have finished reading."

I now waited a good five minutes until she finally nodded her head.

"Excellent, Aliza! You are doing very well!.... Now please return the book to the place you took it from.... Although you are leaving the book behind...you will remember precisely the story you just read.... Once the book is back on the shelf...make your way out of the library building.... Nod your head when you are outside...."

I then slowly brought her out of the trance state. She blinked her eyes and stretched. I waited for her to focus her eyes on me.

"Hello!" I said with a smile. "Welcome back. How was your journey?"

"Strange," she said, "very strange. I read the story of something that happened about twenty-four years ago. I don't know why that memory came up. I haven't thought about it in years."

"If your subconscious mind brought up this memory, there is a good reason for it," I assured her. "Do you feel comfortable telling me about it?"

Once again, I wanted her to feel in control of the situation and not pressured to do something she did not want to do. The memory might have been very personal; if she did not want to share it, I would respect her decision.

"Oh, I have no problem telling you about it," she said. "I just can't understand why this is what came up."

"Well, let me hear the story exactly as it happened, and we'll figure out what it is trying to tell us."

"OK. Twenty-four years ago, when Shimon was four years old, I went with him and my three-month-old baby daughter to visit my mother in Canada. My husband stayed home as he couldn't leave work. My mother had never seen either of the children, as she was elderly and did not travel by plane.

"We had a wonderful time until...." She choked up and found it hard to continue. I handed her some tissues and waited silently, allowing her time to compose herself.

"Sorry. I couldn't control myself," she said after a short while.

"That's quite alright, Aliza. Take as much time as you need."

"As I said, we had a wonderful time until...one day, my baby did not wake up...." She wiped her eyes and blew her nose before continuing. I took this time to compose myself from the shock of hearing her sad story.

"The doctor said it was SIDS, Sudden Infant Death Syndrome,[i] and had nothing to do with me. He assured me that these things happen unexpectedly and there was no way I could have prevented it."

"That is quite true," I said compassionately. "Many mothers blame themselves for this, something that was completely out of their control."

"The police came, to check that there was no abuse involved. That was very upsetting because they bothered me with their questions when I only wanted to be alone and mourn. But the doctor said it was the law and we had to do it.

"I called my husband and he said we must bury her near where we lived. I booked new tickets and brought her home the next day."

"Who traveled with you and Shimon?" I asked.

"My nephew and his wife. My husband met us at the airport, and we went to the cemetery from there."

"How did Shimon react to this?"

"I don't think he really understood. He didn't ask any questions, and he didn't cry."

"Did you explain to him what happened?"

"No, I couldn't bear to do anything. My mother took care of him."

"Did you talk to him on the plane?"

"I couldn't think about anything but my pain. I was also afraid my husband might blame me in some way. Shimon was so quiet that I almost forgot that he was there."

"Did he come to the *levayah*?"

She shook her head in the negative.

"Did you talk to him about it once you felt a little better?"

"No. I couldn't talk about Pessy for months. I was in too much shock. But Shimon seemed fine. He never asked me any questions, so I never brought the subject up with him. I didn't think it was necessary."

"Who was taking care of Shimon during the time that you were in deep shock?" I wanted to know.

"Um...my husband, my sisters...whoever was around."

My mind was rapidly forming a theory about what had caused Shimon to become so closed and noncommunicative. I was quite sure that this sudden death in the family was just as traumatic for Shimon as it had been for his mother. It seemed, though, that Aliza had not made the connection yet. I would try to nudge her gently there until she would see it for herself.

"I believe that this story holds the key to Shimon's present behavior." I paused to let the words sink in and paid close attention to her rapidly changing expressions. "I don't want you to think that I am merely being inquisitive, but I need to know a bit more about what was going on. Is it all right if I ask you some more questions?"

"Sure. Go ahead. I certainly want to get to the bottom of it."

"I believe we will. We're getting closer all the time. So, you told me that as a young child Shimon was talkative and outgoing. What kind of emotions did he express toward his baby sister?"

Aliza was quiet for almost a minute, with her head bent low. Finally, she straightened up, looked me in the eye, and said in a hushed voice, "He loved her, loved her very much. He talked to her and would turn the mobile for her. She even laughed for him sometimes and that made him very happy. Whenever she cried, he pulled me to her and made me take care of her. Or he would rock her pram. The first thing he did when he came home from nursery school was to run to her and talk or play with her."

I used my gentlest tone of voice with my next question. "How do you think Shimon felt when Pessy literally disappeared?"

She simply stared at me without saying a word and her eyes filled with tears. I wanted to alleviate her discomfort, her guilt.

"I realize that you were incapable of thinking about Shimon's feelings when you were so engulfed in pain. It's totally understandable. There was no way you could have focused on Shimon's pain when you were so overwhelmed."

"But why didn't he cry?" she wanted to understand. "Why didn't he ask me what happened?"

"I can only guess, but I believe he was afraid. The police came, there must have been people coming and going, maybe an ambulance arrived with its siren blaring; there must have been a lot of noise. He probably was frightened out of his wits. And if he wanted to speak to you, you weren't available. Maybe your mother or the others who took care of him did not let him come to you. Maybe he did ask you questions, and you simply did not hear him. Maybe he asked someone who told him to be quiet. Maybe he was frozen into silence. Maybe he cried at night into his pillow but not in front of you, thinking that you would be even more upset by seeing him cry. Maybe he blamed himself for what happened, as often young children do when they don't understand what's going on.

"There could be so many logical reasons for why he never said anything. But once he got the message that it was not the right thing for him to express his feelings, and that there was no one around who could make him feel better, he might have learned that expressing feelings is futile. If he could not communicate at a time like that, when it was so important for him to find out what happened, then why would he consider communicating to people in the days following that incident? Simply put, his subconscious mind got a message that when something scary takes place, you don't talk about it or want to know what happened. Just push it out of your mind and suppress your feelings because no one will help you with them anyway. And once that became his new pattern, he got used to not communicating in any type of situation, scary or otherwise. Does this make sense?"

Aliza nodded her head vigorously. "When you put it that way, it certainly does. I never thought of any of this before."

"You said you didn't have this memory for years, and when it did arise you must have felt overwhelmed with emotion. It's quite understandable why you never attached any importance to it concerning Shimon's behavior. However, your subconscious mind did understand its importance in relation to Shimon, and that's why it brought it up now when we asked it to. It really has all the answers."

"So what do I do now?" she asked in desperation. "Is there any way for me to fix the damage that was done then?"

"There's a lot you can do. And this will be the focus of the next phase of your therapy. With Hashem's help, you will notice small but steady changes in his relationship with you. But first, I want to be sure that you forgive yourself. I want you to know that you did the very best you could under the circumstances and with the tools you had then. That will be the foundation for the work we do that follows. Does this make sense?"

"I trust your judgment. Do whatever you think should be done."

"Good. So with your permission, let us begin."

I instructed her to make herself comfortable in the chair and put her into a fairly deep trance. Before we began the therapeutic work, I wanted to be sure she felt safe.

"Is there someone from the present, past, or even the distant past…that you know who is very wise and caring?…. Someone who has your best interest in mind?"

She thought for a moment and then answered slowly, a sign that she was in trance.

"One of my teachers in seminary, Rebbetzin Ashlag…. She always helped me out when I had a problem…. She took good care of me."

"Excellent…. I am now inviting Rebbetzin Ashlag to accompany us on our journey…. She will want to join us…as she has your best interest in mind…. Give me a little nod of your head…to let me know when she is here."

It did not take long for Aliza to nod her head.

"Good…. Aliza, thank the Rebbetzin for coming."

After a small pause, I continued speaking, "Rebbetzin Ashlag…will you please join Aliza as she travels back in time…and keep her safe and protected?"

I was silent for a moment and then asked, "What did she say, Aliza?"

"She said…she is happy to come with me…to keep me safe and protected."

"Excellent…. The two of you will go down the road back in time…and my voice will accompany you."

I then proceeded to have them travel the road back in time until they came to the incident twenty-four years earlier in which Pessy had died. I brought her to the moment before she discovered her life-less infant. I had the Rebbetzin put her arm around Aliza's shoulder in a warm embrace and together they approached the crib.

"Rebbetzin Ashlag...please help Aliza through this very difficult time...and let her know how completely blameless she is in what is taking place.... Aliza, you can pick Pessy up.... You are not alone now.... You can experience everything as it is happening...but now feel the comfort...and feel safe and protected...."

I was silent for several minutes as Aliza envisioned her traumatic experience of the past. Her tears did come, which I anticipated, but I knew that she felt her pain in a safe and protected way as she imagined the Rebbetzin comforting her with wisdom and compassion.

After an appropriate amount of time, I began speaking. "How do you feel, Aliza, with the Rebbetzin at your side?"

"I'm in a lot of pain...but I know I'll get through this.... The Rebbetzin helped me understand that Pessy's death had absolutely nothing to do with my mothering...with how I took care of her.... It is just that Hashem sometimes decides...that things should happen for reasons we don't understand.... She said that Pessy's *neshamah* had a *tikkun*...and fulfilled its purpose...in the short time it was here.... She said I could feel proud...of how well I took care of her...while she was here.... The best part was...how she held me...and let me cry on her shoulder....

"She also assured me that my husband would not be angry...or blame me in any way.... He would completely understand that a crib death...sometimes just happens...and the doctors don't know why...."

"I'm so happy that she is here for you," I said, speaking softly. "She really is wise and caring.... And she can help you in so many ways...."

I let the words sink in before continuing. "I know you are overwhelmed...and cannot think about Shimon...and his pain at this time.... How does that make you feel?"

"I'm feeling guilty about that.... I know he needs some comfort too."

"The Rebbetzin seems to be very wise.... Talk to her about it.... And ask her what you can do...to help Shimon once you are feeling better.... She will be able to guide you...."

I allowed Aliza a lengthy conversation in her imagination with the Rebbetzin. I then asked, "What did the Rebbetzin tell you?"

"She told me I must not feel guilty.... She explained that in the state of shock I was in...it was quite impossible for me...to take care of Shimon.... This was something that Hashem decided...Shimon must go through...for reasons we cannot understand.... But she said that now...that I am feeling better...I can talk to him about what happened.... It doesn't matter how old he is now...it's not too late to talk about it.... I must let him know how sorry I feel...that I could not take care of him then...and even ask his forgiveness...but it was not because I did not love him...or did not care about him.... I just couldn't relate to him...because of the great anguish I was in.... But I want to make it up to him now.... I want to help him in any way that I can...."

I told Aliza that she could begin the process right then of making amends and helping her son. I told her to go with the Rebbetzin and find Shimon and hold and comfort him. Doing this in her mind would prepare the way for the conversations that she needed to initiate with Shimon sometime soon.

I knew that if she could speak to him and comfort him in her imagination during trance, it would serve as a practice session for the conversations she would have in her waking state. I realized that she would need a lot of courage to do that and the more she practiced in her mind, the easier it would be to accomplish in the real world.

After several moments, I asked Aliza to tell me what had happened.

"When I came to Shimon...I could see he was angry and didn't want to talk to me.... When I came close, he ran away.... I don't know what to do!" She was very upset.

"Don't worry, Aliza.... It's OK.... He is expressing his frustration and pain.... But it's good for him to express himself instead of being stoic.... As time passes, he will see how sincere you are and will change his response to your overtures.... For now, let the Rebbetzin go to him and take care of him.... She'll explain to him what he needs to know, and she will begin the process for him to open up to you.... It's good that she is here with you today...."

In this way, I took the burden off her shoulders, allowing the Rebbetzin to deal with the situation. After Aliza reported that the Rebbetzin had been successful in calming Shimon down and comforting him somewhat, I felt it was time to end the session. I repeated in several different ways that we had begun the process of opening up communication between mother and son and that the changes would be apparent slowly but surely. Any resistance on Shimon's part was understandable and with patience and much love his resistance would melt away.

I ended on a positive note. "How happy you must feel, Aliza…that finally, after all these years…you are taking steps to undo the hurt…that Shimon suffered then…. I believe that you…will take on this challenge seriously…and with energy."

I had Aliza thank the Rebbetzin for being there for her and helping. They then parted, with the understanding that they would meet again.

I brought her out of trance and said very casually, "How do you feel?"

She looked at me with wide open eyes. "Amazing! That was unbelievable! But will Shimon want to talk to me?"

"Sure he will! But slowly; it'll be a tiny step after a tiny step. We'll do more sessions with you talking to him, with and without the Rebbetzin, and before you know it, you'll be actually doing it in the flesh. Remember: 'What you can conceive you can achieve!'"

I awaited our next session with niggling impatience, curious as to what it would produce. Aliza came into the room, her facial expression quite animated.

"Welcome, Aliza," I said warmly, as she settled into her seat. "How was your week?"

"All I could think about was our session and how I would manage to get myself to speak to Shimon about Pessy dying…. I also did quite a bit of crying. It was hard to sleep some nights."

"I think that's quite understandable. Did you remember to use your relaxation exercises during this time?"

"I'm sorry," she said sheepishly, "I totally forgot about them. I probably would have slept better had I done so, but...."

"It's OK Aliza. Reexperiencing losing Pessy is quite traumatic, let alone having to worry about helping Shimon overcome his trauma. It's hard to remember how to calm yourself when you're going through that. But I encourage you to use these tools. When you are relaxed you not only feel better; your thinking becomes clearer and you then are able to make better decisions. It will help you bring about the healing you wish to achieve.

"Yes, of course. Maybe I'll remember this week."

"Would you like to ask me anything about last week's session?"

"Everything was so real, and it all made so much sense.... How long do you think it will take me to actually speak to Shimon in real life?"

"Let's leave it open and fluid, without feeling pressured to attain a specific goal," I said. "This is not something you can rush; just let it unfold in its own way."

She nodded in understanding.

"So, shall we begin?"

The session went better than I anticipated. Most of it took place in the recesses of Aliza's mind, with barely a need for my coaching.

Aliza told me afterward that the Rebbetzin was there in the background, guiding her in her interactions with Shimon, giving her the strength and wisdom she sorely needed. And although the child was hesitant at first, Aliza was able to coax him, with toys and candies, to come with her to the playground. There they played together as any carefree mother and child would. It had the effect of melting Shimon's resistance. He was able to show his mother real affection and reverted to being the happy, outgoing little boy that he had once been. Taking her cues from the Rebbetzin, Aliza got the courage to ask Shimon if he missed Pessy.

"He didn't answer and ran off to the monkey bars," she told me. "Hanging upside down and swinging violently back and forth he yelled, 'Why didn't you take care of her? Why didn't you take her to the hospital? Don't all mommies keep their babies safe?'"

She stopped talking, overcome with emotion.

"What did you tell him?" I asked softly.

She looked up, her eyes moist. "I told him everything the Rebbetzin had told me. Those lofty thoughts made sense to me, but I don't know if they did to Shimon. He didn't say anything but came down from the monkey bars. I embraced him in a big hug, and we cried on each other's shoulders."

This session was the first of several in which Aliza was able to encourage the child Shimon to express his feelings, especially his anger, and to ask her questions about what had happened. Each time, she emerged from the session uplifted. She told me that the relationship between herself and Shimon had improved considerably over the past few weeks and I knew that before long she would have the resources to broach the subject of Pessy to the "real" Shimon.

Aliza came in one day shining and I knew that what we had been waiting for had transpired. She wasted no time in telling me about it.

"I was reading in the living room last night, waiting up for Shimon to come home from a date. He got in just past eleven o'clock and I called to him to join me. I asked him how the date had gone. Instead of his usual terse answer he started telling me all about the girl, what he liked about her and what he didn't. He ended with saying that he really didn't think he'd continue seeing her. I simply said that I trusted his judgment.

"He was in a mellow mood and was sharing with me in a way that he hadn't done in a long time. I suddenly felt the urge to speak about what was really on my mind.

"'You know, Shimon,' I said, 'I've been wanting to ask you something for ever so long, I just never found the right time to do it. Do you want to go to sleep, or would you like to spend some time talking with me?'

"He said, sure he'd like to talk to me. I figured the best way to go about it would be to tell the truth and say that I had been having sessions to help me with my anxiety. I said that one of the things that surfaced was some unfinished business of the past. He looked at me questioningly and then I just said it, 'It's about the time Pessy died.' He didn't say anything so I continued. 'I got the feeling that you were hurt or frightened and that I didn't take care of you properly at that time.' He looked down, still without saying anything. I could tell that he was moved."

"Sounds like you did a great job," I said, "allowing him time to digest what you were saying. What happened after that?"

"I imagined the Rebbetzin whispering in my ear and telling me what to do. It gave me the courage to say, 'Shimon, I want to let you know why I didn't talk to you and try to comfort you at that time. I want to replay the scene and take care of you now in a way that I was unable to do then.'

"He remained silent but after a few minutes lifted his head and I could see tears in his eyes. We both broke down, letting the suppressed emotion of years come out. Once we calmed down, I made tea for us both and then we had the most gratifying talk, almost like I had with you in session. We spoke for close to two hours and then Shimon said something that I had never imagined in my wildest dreams that he would say."

"What was that?"

"He said he wanted to go to Pessy's *kever* with me. He had never been there, refusing to go on the *yahrtzeits* with us, and he didn't know exactly where she was buried. We decided to go next week on my day off from work. I can't believe this is happening! It's more than I could ever have hoped for!"

"You put in the work, Aliza, and the tears and prayers," I said with an encouraging smile, "and now you are reaping the rewards."

I myself was amazed at how wonderfully things had progressed. But I cautioned her with a few words of advice. "Probably Shimon would like to be alone at such a momentous time, so be sure to give him his privacy."

Aliza was afraid of becoming too emotional, and we concluded the session with visualizing the graveside scene. Rehearsing in her mind what might take place in the cemetery would enable her to be more in control when she was actually there. She told me that the Rebbetzin had "come with her" to the cemetery and that had strengthened her immeasurably. She said she felt ready for this next challenge.

Aliza later reported that the visit to Pessy's *kever* had acted as a catharsis for both of them. She said that Shimon made numerous visits there on his own, and slowly he turned into the outgoing person he had once been. And their relationship continued to blossom.

At our last session, Aliza promised to update me on her and Shimon's situation. About a half a year later she let me know that Shimon had finally found his soul mate. What could be a greater delight than to see the happy couple create their own *bayis ne'eman b'Yisrael*.

Zelda Neuman

Zelda lived in a small village in the Upper Galilee. The hilly topography made driving a precarious business, not for the fainthearted. It was a common sight to see vehicles swerving around the steep twists and curves of the roads.

Zelda came to me because she was petrified when riding the bus. Most days her husband would bring her to work, driving slowly as per her instructions. But on the occasions when he was unable to, she had no option but to take the bus, and would arrive at work an emotional wreck. Each time she was forced to make use of public transportation, she was quite convinced that she would not survive the ordeal. She wanted help with her panicky feelings of imminent disaster so that she could ride the bus normally.

I wanted to know if she had had any prior mishaps with driving or if she had been in an accident. She replied in the negative.

"Tell me what is happening on your ride that makes you feel so afraid," I said.

"The bus drivers are crazy," she announced adamantly. "They fly around the sharp curves and make the bus rock. It feels like the bus might turn over."

"Please tell me the feelings, the emotions that come up, on those bus rides."

"I feel scared...helpless...overwhelmed...panicky.... I'm afraid I might die."

"Are you frightened like this when driving on a straight road?"

She thought for a minute before answering. "Actually, no. I might feel somewhat nervous, but I certainly don't have that feeling of danger."

"Is this fear of danger only when driving on the hilly roads in your area?

"No. It can be on any hilly or curvy road. It happens when the bus rocks from side to side and I get the feeling that it's going to tumble over. I get so panicky that I feel I might pass out."

"Did you feel this way always, or did this fear start at some point?"

"As a kid I never had a problem. I loved going on the roller coaster and other scary rides. It started much later."

"Please, try to remember when it started. This is very important."

She furrowed her brow in concentration as she did an internal search for the answer to my query. When she finally turned to me, she appeared defeated.

"I know it started after I got married, because I remember a *Chol Hamoed* trip to an amusement park when I already had two small children. I clearly remember having a great time on the adult rides, when I left the little ones in my husband's care. But that was about ten years ago, and I can't put my finger on when it actually started."

"Don't worry," I said. "Although your conscious mind cannot help you out with the answer, your subconscious mind can. It knows the exact time and date of when and why this started. But at least we've reduced the amount of time we need to examine before beginning our therapeutic work."

"What do you mean?" she wanted to understand more fully.

"Your subconscious mind does not forget anything related to your life. It has a library of information all about you from the moment of your conception. What we need to do is to access that repository of information to discover when your fear of riding on hilly, curvy roads began and then to discover why. The answer is there, inside of you. And the solution to the problem is there as well."

"Oh," she said simply. "How do you do that?"

"Using hypnosis, we can ask your subconscious mind to bring up that information."

"Does it always comply with your requests? Can't it refuse to let you know?"

"If it trusts that I am doing whatever I am doing for your ultimate benefit, it will. If for some reason your subconscious mind feels that my knowing this information—or even you knowing it—might not be beneficial to you, it might not cooperate."

"How do you get my subconscious mind to trust you?" Zelda was persistent in her quest for clarity.

"That is up to the skill of the hypnotherapist," I replied with a smile. "There is an art involved with hypnotherapy, not merely a technique. If your subconscious mind does not trust me, believe me, we will get nowhere."

"What happens when I'm in hypnosis?" she wanted to know.

"I gently guide you into a trancelike state, as though you are daydreaming. You won't be asleep and you will clearly hear what I say to you. You might even hear the telephone ringing, but it will just be background noise and will not get your attention. You will be focused on my voice and on your inner experience. Sometimes I will be talking to your conscious mind and sometimes I'll talk to your subconscious mind, almost as though I were talking to two people."

"OK. So let's see how skilled you are," was her blunt reply.

I did not feel as though she was challenging me, but rather, that she was really curious to see what I could do to alleviate her predicament.

"With Hashem's help, we'll get to the bottom of this," I said, with a voice full of confidence. "Every problem has a solution. Are you ready to begin?"

"Absolutely! I'm sick and tired of going through torture whenever I ride the local buses. I want to get over it already!"

"And, *b'siyata d'Shmaya*, you will."

I began speaking slower and using my "hypno" voice, as I wished to induce trance in an indirect manner. "You know, I'd like to compliment your subconscious mind...for doing such a good job at protecting you.... It really works hard...in doing what it believes is best for you.... And sometimes as your life situation changes...it's important to update the techniques...that your subconscious mind uses...to keep you safe.... And I believe that your subconscious mind...is ready to do that now...because you have been suffering...a bit too much...in the current situation...and adjustments need to be made at this time.... And your subconscious mind is quite aware...that some changes are necessary now...."

I continued with my "hypnotic patter," nudging her gently into a trance state. When her eyes closed on their own, without my asking her to close them, I knew she was in hypnosis.

"And as you sink down...into that comfortable state...of relaxation...and allowing yourself to go there...by simply floating down deeper...you feel safe and relaxed...safe and protected.... And you can imagine a bubble surrounding you...a bubble of white light...that completely envelopes you...to keep you safe.... This is your bubble of protection from Hashem...filled with a Divine white light.... And you know that here...you are completely safe...."

My intuition was telling me that she might be suffering from some trauma of the past. As I wished to bring that memory to the surface, I first needed to create a sense of safety for her. Without that feeling of safety, her subconscious mind might resist bringing up the traumatic situation to her consciousness. I continued talking a bit longer, repeating the message in various ways, until she let me know with a nod of her head that she felt completely safe.

"And now that you are totally safe...and nothing can harm you...not your feelings...not the pictures in your mind...not even old memories...nothing at all...I'd like you to imagine yourself...sitting on that rocking, swaying bus.... Be there now...inside your bubble of white light...that is keeping you safe...and feel the jolting movements shaking you around....Feel it happening now...and if it reminds you of something else.... Tell me if you felt scared...help-less...overwhelmed...panicky...afraid you might die...if you felt any of that before...at a different time...in a different situation."

I remained silent as she sat quietly for a few minutes. Her face suddenly tensed up, as though she had some shocking revelation.

"Oh! Yes, I did." She spoke haltingly, almost gasping as though she were reliving the experience. "When we lived in Haifa...I'm in a building on the top floor.... There is a café...on the street level.... Suddenly there is this tremendous boom...and the whole building is shaking.... I feel it rocking from side to side.... I'm thrown down...on the floor.... I think I'm dying...."

She stopped speaking, overcome by the memory. I suppressed a small gasp upon hearing her terrifying words. I controlled my emotions before speaking again.

"And you are safe inside your bubble of white light." I wanted to re-mind her of that, to let her know that she need not fear. "You know you are not dying...for you are here now...telling me the tale...and you are safe....What happens after you fall?"

"I pick myself up....I'm covered in plaster from the ceiling...but I am not hurt.... I walk downstairs.... The café is blown up.... Devastation...blood...dead bodies...wounded people screaming...."

She began crying and I gave her some tissues. She wiped her eyes and then began speaking again.

"I run out fast.... I sit on the bench.... The ambulance comes.... A man wants to put me in the ambulance.... 'No, I'm OK, I'll take a taxi home'.... I go home.... I sleep for two days...."

"Very good.... You sleep for two days and you recuperate.... The rocking, swaying building did not harm you...it only frightened you.... Did you slowly stop thinking about what happened...and go back to normal living?"

"I spoke to a psychologist.... She helped me.... After a while I stopped thinking about it...."

"How old were you...when that café exploded?"

"Twenty-seven."

"I'd like you to go deeper now Zelda...five...four...three...two... one....Go back to that rocking, swaying building...inside your bubble of white light...safe and protected.... Feel those feelings again...scared...helpless...overwhelmed...panicky...afraid you might die....You can confront those feelings...because they won't harm you...just experience them again...like an objective observer.... Feel them now.... Are these feelings new...or familiar?"

"Familiar...."

"That's right...familiar....You felt this way...another time...once before.... Go back now...back in time...five...four...three...two... one.... Go back to that other time...an earlier time...when you felt those feelings...."

She was there immediately, without needing to introspect.

"I'm at the doctor's in Jerusalem.... I leave the office to take the bus home.... I forgot my umbrella...I go back for it.... I run to the bus stop...but the bus drives off.... There is a big explosion.... The ground shakes.... I fall down.... The bus is burning!" She began cry-ing again, and used the tissues she was holding to blow her nose.

Once again, with a supreme effort, I controlled my emotions, and continued to speak calmly.

"And *baruch Hashem*, you missed the bus...." I stated, lest she forgot this important point. "Hashem protected you then...and always pro-tects you.... As you feel these feelings...when the bus explodes...and you fall down...are these feelings new or familiar?"

"New."

We had reached the first time she had felt that way, the first event that began the process of creating her present panic, the initial sensitizing event or ISE. Often there are many situations going back many years in a person's life that act together to create a phobia or an extreme and unrealistic fear. As we learned above, it is important to reach the ISE, the first one, for if the practitioner only neutral-izes subsequent events the therapy is incomplete, and the phobia may return.

"That's right...new.... This is the first time you feel like this...overwhelmed and scared...afraid you might die...when the ground you stand on...or anything your feet are standing on...rocks and shakes...and sways.... The first time.... How old are you?"

"Twenty-five...."

"When you went to the amusement park...on *Chol Hamoed*...was that before the bus you missed exploded?"

"Yes...before...."

Within two years, Zelda had experienced two terror attacks in which she miraculously had been unharmed physically, but which had caused her to be deeply traumatized. Her subconscious mind had prevented her from thinking of those incidents in order to protect her from feeling the emotional pain she had suffered on those occasions. However, when the physical feelings of rocking and swaying turned up in her life, they caused her to reexperience the rocking and swaying she had felt during the bombings and caused her to once again suffer the emotions that had overwhelmed her at that time. It all made perfect sense.

In one session, just by discovering its root cause, we had accomplished a major piece of the healing work Zelda would need to undergo in order to be rid of her bus-riding fear. Although history could not be rewritten and the trauma Zelda had undergone could not be undone, it was possible to change her feelings relating to the "rocking and swaying" that took place in her daily life. I was fairly certain that in a few short sessions of hypnosis and mind exercises, Zelda would no longer associate rocking and swaying with terror bombings and death. With *siyata d'Shmaya*, Zelda's perception of those feelings would be turned into something that was pleasant or, at the worst, something a bit annoying. My plan for her transformation was already gelling in my mind.

"Remember, Zelda...how much you enjoyed the rides in the amusement parks?.... It was so much fun.... Even though the rides you were on...rocked and swayed...and shook...and made you scream in fright...you loved them so much.... I'd like you to feel the rocking and swaying and being shaken around on your favorite amusement park ride.... You're there with your husband or with a friend and having such a good time.... You know it is safe even if it seems scary.... It's so much fun...that you even laugh out loud sometimes.... Have a good joy ride now...in this safe and fun-filled amusement park.... Be there now...."

I waited silently as her changing facial expressions let me know that she was having a very positive experience. She did actually laugh out loud several times.

"Very good!.... Excellent.... I'm so glad you're having a great time.... Feel that pleasure...of a great time...filling you up...and when that happens, I'd like you to press the thumb and forefinger of your right hand together to form a circle.... Every time you feel the pleasure of your amusement park rides you will press your two fingers together the way I described. This is called the 'anchor,' and when you activate your anchor...you bring up and feel the pleasure of those amusement park rides...."

I spent several minutes reviewing the anchor exercise with her until she was able to experience the joyful feelings on her own whenever she did it. I then slowly brought her out of hypnosis.

She opened her eyes and smiled at me. "I guess you do know how to get my subconscious mind to trust you," she exclaimed emphatically. "That was unreal!"

"I couldn't agree with you more," I replied. "I am often surprised by what that subconscious mind can come up with. It knows more about you than you know about yourself!"

"Yes, indeed. I hadn't thought about those terror attacks for quite a while. After my sessions with the psychotherapist, they were pushed into the back of my mind."

"That is quite understandable. If reliving those terror attacks is too painful to you, your subconscious will try to repress the memory so that you don't reexperience the pain. That's exactly what I mean by your subconscious mind doing for you what it feels is in your best interest."

"So why did the memory come up now? Thinking about it still shakes me up an awful lot." She looked off into the distance and her facial pallor clearly indicated the distress she must have been feeling.

"Have a drink of water," I said as I handed her a glass. "When you finish drinking, take a few deep breaths. That's right. You'll feel better in a moment."

It didn't take long before a smile returned to her face.

"Yes, I do feel better. So tell me, why did the memory come up now?"

"Simple! I explained to your subconscious mind that the old techniques it was using to keep you safe were outdated and needed to be upgraded for your ultimate benefit. Your subconscious mind trusted me enough to accept my suggestion and I was able to bring up the memories that are causing your present distress."

"You make it sound simple, but I imagine it takes some skill to do that."

"Yes, it takes much training and a lot of *siyata d'Shmaya*," I responded. "If you want to be the best version of yourself so that you can serve Hashem better, He will surely help you attain that goal. He certainly saved your life quite openly on two occasions!"

"Oh yes! We made a separate *seudas hodaah* for each time I was *zocheh* to a miraculous salvation!"

I instructed her to practice the anchor exercise at least five times every day. I wanted it to become second nature for her to bring up pleasurable feeling—so easy that she would be able to do it even in her sleep.

The next part of Zelda's therapy would be quite different. I believed she needed additional strategies for when she was on a shaky bus ride. I wanted her to have a stronger form of distraction to get her through the ride in a relatively calm state.

At our next session, I asked her what she did while riding the bus. She said she felt impelled to keep her eyes glued upon the bus driver, as though by fixing her gaze on him she could somehow control his driving. And, therefore, she would then recite whichever chapters of *Tehillim* she knew by heart.

"I'm happy you know *Tehillim* by heart because the next technique I'm going to teach you will keep your hands busy, and you won't be able to hold a *sefer Tehillim*. What I'm going to teach you is really important and will enable you to ride the bus calmly."

I taught her to twiddle her fingers in an intricate manner.

"I want you to press the thumb of your right hand to the forefinger of your left hand and spread your other fingers wide. The fingers of your right hand should point up and the thumb of your left hand should point down."

She followed my instructions.

"Now I want you to take the thumb of your left hand which is pointing down and swivel your hand around in an upward direction and then touch it to the forefinger of your right hand. These fingers will now be positioned above the other fingers that are touching. Good. Now separate the right thumb from the left forefinger, swivel your hands around until the separated fingers point up, and then touch the thumb of the right hand to the forefinger of the left hand. Good. Now separate the fingers that are touching, which are positioned below the other fingers, and swivel your hands around until the fingers are on top and touch the thumb and forefinger together. Continue doing this over and over again."

The instructions were hard to follow and she got confused. This caused her to laugh in embarrassment. But I encouraged her and with my guidance she finally got the hang of it. I told her to keep repeating the touching, separating, and swiveling of fingers over and over, until she could do it on her own without my instructions.

"Wow!" Zelda exclaimed. "That is some exercise. I'm actually sweating, and I feel like I had a real workout."

"It will become very easy with practice," I assured her. "In the short while you've been doing it, you've improved an awful lot."

"What's the point of this?" she wanted to know.

"In many healing modalities, there is deep meaning to the concepts of right and left. In this exercise you have full control of your fingers on the right and the left and are using both in synchronization. How this affects you exactly is beyond my understanding, but it might have to do with synchronizing the right and left hemispheres of the brain. Believe me, if you do this while riding the bus and saying *Tehillim* by heart, you will discover that the ride seems totally harmless—uncomfortable, maybe—but harmless."

I knew that she would be concentrating so fully on doing the exercise correctly that her mind would not be able to focus on her fearful thoughts. By doing this in combination with using her anchor to bring up pleasant feelings, I believed she could hold on to a certain measure of calm. At least that was my hope. Of course, there was also the possibility that she would stop twiddling her fingers and revert to her old pattern of anxiety and panic

"Do you know anybody who did this and got results?" Zelda's voice broke into my thoughts.

"Some of my teachers used this technique with their clients with great results. The only way for you to know if it works is for you is to try it out."

I ended the session with a hypnotic trance in which we repeatedly reviewed the anchor technique. She experienced herself using it in various situations in order to bring up the pleasant feelings associated with rocking and swaying. I also had her experience herself riding on a rocking and swaying bus and using the "twiddle the fingers" technique as she said *Tehillim*. I had her imagine herself laughing happily as she succeeded in doing the intricate finger movements.

I brought her out of hypnosis and asked, "How do you feel?"

"Good, pretty good. I felt a sense of satisfaction doing that funny finger twiddle."

"Was the bus swaying very much?" I wanted to know.

She looked at me quizzically and then laughed. "I really didn't notice!"

"Great! That's exactly what will happen when you get on a real live bus. Tomorrow you're going to find that out."

"What do you mean?" Zelda sounded apprehensive.

"Tomorrow, *b'siyata d'Shmaya*, you and your husband will do a little exercise together. In case it doesn't work out for you tomorrow, you'll do it the next day. Your husband should drive you to the bus stop, while you activate your anchor and fill up with those happy feelings. Then you will get on the bus and ride for one bus stop only. During the ride you will twiddle your fingers and say *Tehillim*. Your husband will follow along in the car. You will get off the bus after one stop and he will drive you home or to wherever you want to go. At home, you will celebrate your success at being able to ride the bus calmly. You'll repeat this one-stop bus ride several times. When you come back for your next session, I'll tell you the next step in the process."

"Are you serious? You want me to get on a bus when I don't have to? I'm not ready! We only had two sessions!"

"Two very powerful sessions! This is exactly what I want you to do! The point of your therapy is to get you to be able to ride the bus as anyone else does. The only way to get over your fear is to face it, while helping yourself with the techniques you learned. I can't erase your fear for you. But you have all the tools you need for you to do it yourself. Practice deep breathing and activating your anchor as often as possible. This will give you the calm and the empowerment you need for success.

"When you get on the bus, knowing that your ride is for one stop only and will be over very shortly, you won't feel worried. I assure you that when you twiddle your fingers and say *Tehillim* during the ride, you won't have a problem at all."

"I hope you're right!"

"You can be curious to discover just how right I am."

Of course, I had no way of knowing how things would transpire, but I had to give her the belief that it would turn out as I was predicting. I was actually giving her subliminal messages for her success.

Zelda returned the following week all smiles. Her short bus ride, she said, was "a piece of cake!" I instructed her over the following weeks to increase her ride by one additional stop each time. In hypnosis she would see herself negotiating the ride calmly and peacefully, even being able to read a book or speak on her cell phone.

At some point, it became inconvenient for her husband to come along in the car, and so she started taking the bus back home. Within four weeks, she was riding the bus just as you or I would. And she even stopped twiddling.

5

SINGLE-SESSION TRANSFORMATIONS

Rivky Silver

Sometimes clients need several sessions before achieving their healing, and often, after we stop meeting, they choose to come back for reinforcement of the major changes they've been experiencing. But other times, I've been privileged to witness one-session miracles. This was one of them.

Rivky was four months postpartum when her mother, Leah Green, called me. Her mother was an old acquaintance who had taken childbirth preparation classes with me years earlier.

After exchanging pleasantries, Leah explained her reason for calling. "I'm worried about my daughter Rivky. She had her first baby four months ago."

"Mazel tov! A boy or a girl?"

"A very sweet girl. The baby is fine, but the problem is with Rivky. She has this weird symptom that no one can figure out. It's making us all crazy."

"Please tell me about it," I said, curious as to what this weird symptom was.

"Ever since she had the baby, she sometimes feels as though she is floating above her body. It can come at any time without any apparent reason. She gets very upset when it happens because it feels so strange, so unnatural. She won't go outside, because she's afraid that the feeling might overwhelm her and make her lose control of herself.

"The doctor ran a number of tests and everything came back normal. Since he couldn't figure it out, he decided to give her anti-anxiety medications. They made no difference at all, and so he took her off the drugs. I thought maybe you could help her with relaxation and breathing techniques. What do you think?"

"It certainly wouldn't hurt to try," I answered. "They would make her feel calmer and then she'd feel better and less panicky. I might also be able to get to the root of the problem as I work with her."

"That sounds good. When could you start?"

"Next week."

"Great. The only thing is that you'd have to come to her as she's afraid to go out."

"OK. I'll check my calendar, and let you know when I can be there."

The following week, I arrived at Rivky's house without any preconceived ideas of how I would work with her. I had never heard of a symptom such as this after birth. Since all her lab tests were normal, I was quite sure it had to do with her emotional state. Something had created that strange sensation and she'd become stuck in a loop in which the feeling was created over and over again. I'd have to discover what had caused her initial feeling of floating.

I rang the bell and she opened the door.

"Hello, Mrs. Toporowitch. Thanks for coming." She brought me into the living room where she had put out drinks and cake.

"Mazel tov, Rivky! So how's the baby?"

"*Baruch Hashem*, she's fine, thanks. My mother took her out so we could be undisturbed.

"Excellent, then we can begin straight away. Your mother told me briefly, but I'd like to hear from you what you're feeling."

"OK. It's hard to describe but suddenly I get this weird feeling like I'm floating out of my body, up in the air and looking down. It's so scary that I run to bed, no matter what I'm doing. If no one else is home I'll take the baby to bed with me, but I feel so out of it that I can't take care of her. If she cries, I try to feed her, but I'm not able to get up and change her diaper until the feeling goes away." She sat hunched, twisting the tissue she was holding.

"How long does the feeling last?"

"I don't really know, but I guess about ten or fifteen minutes. Sometimes I manage to fall asleep in bed, and other times I just wait, without focusing on anything. Sometimes I call my husband to come home." She was now shredding the tissue into little pieces.

"When exactly did this start?"

Rivky gazed at the ceiling as she began reliving her memories. "I think the first time I felt it was the day after I came to my mother's house after I left the mother-and-baby convalescent home I'd gone to right from the hospital. And since then it comes and goes whenever it pleases."

"Has this ever happened to you in the past?"

She shook he head in the negative.

"I want you to tell me exactly what happened to you, in great detail, and everything you were feeling from the moment you had the baby."

She began her tale, with quite a bit of emotion, describing a whole series of mini traumas. To begin with, she had a hard time with the breastfeeding; then in the convalescent home she couldn't get any sleep because her roommate was constantly having visitors and talking on the phone. No less annoying was the mosquito that kept her awake the whole night with its infernal buzzing. Finally, on the third day of her stay, her baby developed a fever. That night, the nurse came to let her know.

"I was trying my best to get some sleep when this nurse comes over to me and says, 'Mrs. Silver, your baby has a fever.' I was shocked. I asked her how high it was, and she said 100 degrees Fahrenheit, enough to be concerned.

"'Can something be done to bring the fever down?' I asked her. She said she had given the baby Tylenol to take the fever down. Since they couldn't call the doctor at night, she told me to take the baby to the hospital.

"I was so scared, I almost yelled at her. 'Take the baby to the hospital? All by myself? Are you crazy?' I started to cry.

"She was adamant that they could not take responsibility for a sick baby if they had no doctor on the premises. I jumped out of bed to call my husband and ask him to come over right away. He said I shouldn't wait for him to come, as he was quite a distance away, so I should call my mother and ask her advice. I did that and my mother said I shouldn't go to the hospital but should take a taxi and come to her house. I told the nurse I was going to go to my mother's. She said I had to sign a paper releasing the mother-and-baby home from all responsibility. I packed up my things as quickly as I could, signed the paper she gave me, and called a taxi."

Rivky was talking fast and I could tell she was very agitated as she relived the experience. I tried to keep eye contact with her, but most of the time she was looking off into the distance, as though seeing her memory in her mind's eye.

"The taxi came pretty soon and I got in with my things. The baby was quiet, probably because of the Tylenol. I gave the driver the address, and he started driving really fast. I told him to slow down, but he only flew faster. I was so scared; he was flying at maybe 150 kilometers an hour!"

She started crying at this point. It became hard for her to speak, but she struggled on with her story. "I asked him why he was driving so fast and he said, 'It's late. I want to get home already!' He was flying down that road, flying so fast, flying like someone was chasing him, and I was afraid he'd have an accident."

She wiped her eyes, blew her nose, and managed to compose

herself. "We finally got to my mother's house and I got out of that awful taxi with my poor little baby. The next day my mother took the baby to the doctor and in a few days she was all better. But then this crazy feeling of floating out of my body started. Since then I can't relax; I'm a bundle of nerves."

I knew now where the problem lay. She had used the word "flying" at least five times in her narrative. That was when she became so emotional that she could no longer contain her crying. The feeling of flying had been traumatic for her. Subconsciously she was caught up in this memory loop which caused her to reexperience the feeling repeatedly. She had no conscious understanding of it, nor did she have conscious control over the sensation. Her floating out of her body was her way of expressing that "flying" in a most negative way. I had to give Rivky her control back, the control she had lost when the driver took her on that wild ride.

"Wow, that's some story, Rivky. But with Hashem's help, I'm sure we'll be able to get rid of that feeling, really soon. We'll start with some breathing exercises, which will help you relax and feel more in control."

My voice conveyed a strong sense of confidence in what we were about to do. I didn't want her to think for a moment that there was no help for her.

I taught her a deep-relaxation type of breathing, explaining the science behind it, and how it would enable her to remain calm. I told her to practice her breathing techniques three times daily for a minimum of five minutes, and whenever she felt the floating feeling come on. I then put her into a deep trance and had her visualize herself in an airplane. I told her that she was an experienced pilot and knew exactly how to fly the plane. I had her take the plane up and put it through many maneuvers. I emphasized repeatedly how she felt fully in control of the plane, maneuvering it about easily. We did this for several minutes and then I suggested to her how easy it was for her to bring the plane down. I let the suggestion sink in for several moments. I then told her to bring the plane down, efficiently and easily, in a gentle landing.

While she was still in trance, I asked her, "How did you feel flying that plane?"

"Good."

"It is easy for you to take the plane up...and make maneuvers with it.... How easy is it for you to do that?"

"Very easy."

"It is easy for you to take the plane down.... How easy is it for you to do that?"

Very easy."

"Good.... Now any time you want...you can take the plane up or down, as you wish.... You will continue to do this for the next few days...practicing over and over again your control of the plane.... Every day you will practice flying your plane...taking it up and taking it down....Are you going to do that?"

"Yes."

"How often?"

"Every day."

"Very good.... You are doing...very good."

I repeated my instructions to her again, as repetition is so important in hypnosis, and then brought her out of trance. She appeared very calm.

"How are you feeling?" I asked.

"Good; relaxed."

"You did really well. Do you have any questions?"

"No."

"Now remember to practice the breathing technique at least three times a day and also whenever necessary for the floating feeling. And you will do your visualization of flying your plane at least once a day. You will take the plane up, do whatever you want in the sky, and then bring the plane down, every day at least once or twice a day. OK?"

"OK."

"It's really important that you do this every day. Then, after about five days, call me up to let me know how you are doing. And, if you want, we'll set up another appointment at that time. If you have any questions or notice any changes in the way you feel, you can call me any time."

"OK." I could see she was still somewhat in trance and didn't feel much like talking. I had her drink water, repeated my instructions, and left.

I waited for her call. She didn't call after five days, and not after a week. I was worried, wondering what was happening. I finally called her myself after ten days of waiting.

"Hello, Rivky. How are you? Is everything OK?"

"Hello, Mrs. Toporowitch. Yes, sure, everything is great. The floating feeling is gone!"

"Gone? After how long?"

"Oh, maybe after three days of doing that exercise it was completely gone. So I stopped the exercise and it just never came back."

"Wonderful! Why didn't you call me to let me know?"

"Sorry about that, I'm just so busy with my new baby that I kept on forgetting to call you. I know I should have but...."

"It's OK. You're not the only one. People tend to call when things aren't going well and somehow forget to call when things are going great."

Rivky had had a one-time trauma and it was relatively easy to neutralize it once I discovered the cause. I had assumed she'd need two or three sessions to get over it completely. To my pleasant surprise, she never had a repeat of the floating sensation and I was thrilled that we had achieved a one-session "miracle."

Tamara Sassoon

I had been running a stress-management workshop in Vienna, when, just before its conclusion, a lovely young lady from the group approached me after the other women had left. From the concerned look on her face, I could see she had a problem.

"Bracha, I know you're leaving Vienna soon, but I was wondering if you might be able to help me with something."

"I certainly would love to if I can. Tell me about it."

"I have this intense, overpowering worry about my son. I can't stop worrying and I can't sleep at night because of it."

"Has anything you learned in the workshop been of help to you?" I wanted to know.

"Yes, definitely. The techniques we learned are helpful in lessening the worry about 50 percent. I was hoping that by the end of the workshop it would have become much better. But because the worry is so intense, whatever is left of it is still driving me crazy. I was wondering if you could do a session with me before you leave."

I consulted my appointment book to see if I could fit her in. I knew we would not be able to have more than one session, and this was before there was the option of Zoom or even Skype for further consults. I had no idea as to the cause of her worry. However, sometimes treating the symptom alone could be very effective in alleviating the problem. In other cases, it would be necessary to go deeper and get to the root cause. I figured I could use a powerful method for neutralizing the actual worry without dealing with the reason for it. It might work, or not, but that was all I could offer her.

"I can't promise any results with one session," I said matter-of-factly, "however, we might be surprised. If you like, I can see you this evening."

Tamara arrived promptly for our session. She still had that look of intense concern but thanked me sincerely for making the time to see her.

"It's my great pleasure if I can be of help to you. Now, before we begin, I'd like to know a bit more about this worry. In general, are you a big worrier?"

"No, not more than other people I know. I don't remember ever worrying about something in this way before."

"Good. How long have you been suffering with this worry?

"Only in the last month. Before that I can't recall anything out of the ordinary."

"Great!" I said. I felt our task would be much easier if this was a one-time occurrence for her.

"I'm not even going to ask you what the worry is, because we will focus exclusively on the feelings and not at all on the thoughts concerning it. We will use a guided imagery visualization that I created and have taught for many years, although I did not include it in the workshop you participated in.

"As you have learned, when you imagine something, your subconscious mind can make it feel real to you, as though it were actually happening. The subconscious mind does not work logically or realistically, and what you imagine, no matter how illogical it may be, will be very real to your subconscious mind. If it accepts what we will now do, it will make your worry disappear. But I want you to remember that when you imagine what I tell you to imagine, don't remain within the constraints of logic—let your imagination run away with you and be as fantastic as it wants to be. Is this clear?"

"Yes, it is. But I have a slight problem. When you tell me to visualize something, I can't see it." Tamara looked crestfallen.

"Don't worry about that," I reassured her. "When I say 'imagine' something, you can see, hear, feel, or simply sense that it is there. Let's try something. Close your eyes and imagine an apple. Nod your head when the apple is there."

She nodded.

"Tell me, Tamara, what color is your apple?"

After a moment she responded, "It's yellow."

"Great. Open your eyes. Did you see the yellow apple?"

"No, but I knew it was yellow."

"Perfect! Now you know that you will be able to imagine something, whether or not you actually 'see' it. With practice you will get to see more vividly what your mind imagines."

"That's a relief!" Tamara sighed. "So what am I going to imagine?"

"You will clearly imagine a 'balloon release.' With this visualization your worry will disappear and you will fill up with an emotion that you would rather have. Tell me, Tamara, what do you want to feel instead of worry?"

She thought for several seconds. "I think I want to have *emunah*, lots of *emunah*. Also, acceptance. I want to be able to accept what is, and not agonize over what is not."

"Good. We will call the emotion we are getting rid of 'worry,' and the emotion you wish to have instead is 'acceptance of Hashem's way of taking care of you.' Is that accurate?"

"Yes, exactly, but I want to add that I also want to feel calm and peaceful as I accept Hashem's decision."

"OK, so let's call it '*emunah* enveloped in feelings of calm and peaceful acceptance.' For short, we'll call it '*emunah* with calm and peaceful acceptance.' Is that right?"

"It sounds good."

"One more question, Tamara, do you *really* want to get rid of this worry?"

"Yes! Definitely!" she replied forcibly.

"Is there any reason at all for you to hold onto this worry?" Her answer to this question would reveal to me if there might be any internal resistance to getting rid of the worry.

She did not answer immediately but sat sunk in thought. Finally she asked, "Maybe it helps me do more *hishtadlus* to make things happen if I have this worry?"

"Will your *worry* enable something to happen? Or can you effect change even if you didn't have the worry?" I needed to know what she believed before I continued with the visualization.

"I think if I didn't have any worry at all I would be too passive and not do anything."

"I understand. Most people have a certain amount of worry in difficult situations, and that can be useful in getting them to make the effort needed for them to help themselves. However, if not controlled, worry can become excessive and damaging rather than helpful. When worry is excessive you will not be able to think coherently and you might make mistakes through faulty judgment. In that case, the worry becomes damaging rather than helpful. So, let us now say that you want to get rid of 'excessive worry'—not the normal level of worry but the exaggerated worry that is hurting rather than helping the situation. Makes sense?"

"Yes! That sounds perfect."

"Great. So now we can begin. Make yourself comfortable in the chair and close your eyes. Do not open your eyes, even when I ask you questions and you answer them. I want you to stay with the imagery right up until the time we finish.

"Please focus for a moment on the negative feeling of 'excessive worry' and tell me on a scale of zero to ten how do you feel it, zero meaning you don't have that feeling at all and ten being the greatest possible amount of that feeling."

"I feel it like a ten for sure, maybe even a twenty." Her answer let me know just how distressed she was feeling.

This guided imagery exercise can be done with good results by simply having the client close her eyes, but I wanted Tamara to do it while in hypnosis in order to magnify the effect. I spent a few minutes putting her into a light trance.

"Continue taking those nice, deep relaxing breaths.... Fill your chest and abdomen with oxygen...becoming more relaxed...with every breath that you take.... As you breathe into your abdomen...you notice that a balloon surfaces from within...coming right out of you.... It is not inflated but is suspended in the air opposite you.... Written across the face of this balloon in big, bold, black letters...are the words 'excessive worry'....

"As you continue breathing, you direct the breath toward your stomach...feeling your abdomen rise and fall as you breathe...and imagine that you are exhaling this excessive worry of yours from inside of you right out into the balloon.... As you do this, notice how the balloon is inflating...growing larger and larger.... You continue filling the balloon with your excessive worry...with every out-breath...allowing it to expand and expand.... Do not worry about the balloon bursting.... It won't, for it is a very strong balloon.... The larger the balloon grows...the more of your excessive worry you are emptying out of yourself.... Keep filling it with your excessive worry...until the point where you feel you have filled it as much as you can.... You may have gotten out all of your excessive worry...or maybe only a part of it...and in that case you can continue this exercise tomorrow...and the next day...emptying out even more excessive worry...continuing with this imagery until you have rid yourself of all of your excessive worry.... But now, when you feel that the balloon cannot inflate any larger...when you feel that you have inflated it to the maximum...just nod your head to let me know."

I waited for her head nod, which took some time in coming.

"Tell me, Tamara, how big is the balloon?.... It might be as big as yourself...as big as this room...as big as this building...as big as a mountain...or even as big as all of Vienna...or even larger.... The larger it is, the more excessive worry...you have been able to expel from within.... So, how big is your balloon?"

She spoke slowly, and quietly. "It's as big as all of the Alps."

"Excellent!.... In case you still need to get rid of some more excessive worry...you can carry on doing this whenever you wish.... But now, notice how the balloon rises, just like a helium balloon...trying to fly off into the sky above.... But you realize that it can't...it is tied down.... The balloon can't fly off because it is tied to your wrist with a cord.... Can you feel it tugging at your wrist...pulling on it...as it wants to fly up?"

I waited for her response. After a second, she gave me a small head nod.

"Tell me, do you want the balloon to fly off into the heavens...so that you can rid yourself of it, with all your excessive worry that it contains?"

"Yes."

"What can you do to allow that balloon to fly up and away?"

"I'll cut the cord."

"That's right.... Imagine picking up a pair of scissors and cutting right through the cord.... I don't know how difficult or easy it may be for you to cut through the cord.... Just keep on cutting...until you succeed...and the cord is completely cut through.... If you need a bigger tool...like an electric saw...you can take one and use it.... Give me a nod of your head when you cut through...."

After a short pause she nodded.

"Very good.... Now, what's happening to the balloon...this helium balloon?"

I needed to hear from her that she saw or felt the balloon flying off. I never want to put words in a client's mouth, for then I cannot know for sure if that's what she is actually experiencing.

"The balloon is flying up."

"Excellent!.... Now, watch that balloon rising upward into the blue sky...rising higher and higher and becoming smaller and smaller....What does it look like now?"

"It's becoming so small."

"How small is it?.... Can you see it at all?"

"It's just a dot.... It's gone."

"Wonderful.... How good it is to get rid of that balloon...with its contents.... What a relief.... What a heavy load you just let go of.... Feel the sensation of relief and lightness....

"You may even notice that you feel an empty place inside...an emptiness inside where you were holding that excessive worry before.... In nature there are no vacuums...an empty place immediately fills up with something.... If you don't want your excessive worry to return...and fill up that vacuum inside of you...we need to quickly fill that space with something else...something better....

"Now is your opportunity to fill up that empty space inside of you...with 'emunah with calm and peaceful acceptance.' Look up to *Shamayim*.... Hashem has storehouses in Heaven...full of exactly what you need...in plentiful supply.... Imagine that wonderful feeling of 'emunah with calm and peaceful acceptance'...coming down to you from Hashem's storehouse in Heaven...straight from Hashem....

Notice in which way that delicious, special feeling of *emunah* comes down to you.... Is it like raindrops?.... Like rays of light?.... Like waves of energy?.... Notice how Hashem sends it to you.... See, feel, and experience that amazing feeling of *emunah* filling up the void inside of you...not leaving any room for that other feeling to come back.... Feel yourself filling up more and more...with that wonderful new feeling of *emunah* with calm and peacefulness.... Let it warm your insides...with calm and peace."

I paused, as I watched her facial expression transforming.

"Good, very good.... Now just enjoy that new feeling for a moment."

I remained silent for long pause.

"And now you prepare to return to full alertness...full wakefulness...coming back to this room...knowing that you will not be the same person you were...before doing this 'balloon release'.... Take three deep breaths...and open your eyes."

Her eyes were moist and she wiped them with the tissue I handed her. Relief was written all over her face.

"How do you feel, Tamara?"

"Amazing. It's like I'm coming back from another world."

"Have a drink of water." I handed her a glass full and waited till she finished.

"How did you see the *emunah* feeling coming down from Heaven?

"It was like waves of light; soft, blue light in gentle waves."

"Beautiful. Could you feel yourself filling up with it?"

"Definitely! That's the amazing feeling I'm talking about."

"Now, try to bring up the excessive worry as you did when we started. Then you said it felt like a ten or even a twenty. What does it feel like now?"

"Like nothing! It's all gone! It's a zero!"

I was a little skeptical. "Are you sure?"

"I mean it! There is no more worry. I absolutely cannot imagine what I was worried about. I'm feeling that whatever Hashem decides is the right thing for us."

"Do you want to share what the worry was all about? You don't have to if it makes you feel uncomfortable."

"I'm fine with sharing. I was afraid my son would not be accepted to the *yeshiva gedolah* my husband and I had our hearts set on. I think now that it was an ego thing, and that being in that yeshiva is super good for *shidduchim*. I was obsessed with something that I had no control over and didn't really even know if it was the best choice for our Yaakov. And now it seems to me that I was worrying absolutely for nothing. It just doesn't matter anymore. Hashem knows what is best for Yaakov, and whether he is accepted or not into yeshiva X is in His hands. How could I have ever begun to think that I knew better?"

"I'm really happy for you that you got this clarity and peace of mind," I said, as I flashed her a big smile. "I'm sure you'll sleep well tonight."

"Wow, Bracha! This is amazing! I can't believe that in one short hour this transformation could take place. I'm so grateful!"

Bruriya Dunner

At one point, it was my custom to offer the brides in our community the gift of a free relaxation session before their marriage. Often the young women are stressed out from the myriad tasks that need attending to and from sleep deprivation. My one-hour session would teach them techniques for relaxing and creating a positive mindset. The short hypnotic trance they enjoyed would enable them to melt away any accumulated tension or fear. The purpose of my gift was not intended to deal with issues of a complex nature.

Bruriya was a twenty-year-old *kallah*. Her mother called me shortly before the wedding day. I could clearly hear the worry in her voice.

"I'd be very happy to take your offer of a relaxation session for my daughter Bruriya," she said.

"With pleasure," I replied.

"The wedding is in ten days. Could you see her right away?"

"I can see her tomorrow at 5:00 p.m. Does that work out for you?"

"I'll make it work because it's really important that she comes. You see, Bruriya has suddenly got this crazy idea that maybe she made a mistake and this boy is not for her. She's turned into a nervous wreck!"

"Oh dear! How upsetting!" I felt truly concerned. "Does she have any reason for this 'crazy idea'?"

"As much as I question her about it, she can't come up with any explanation. She said it just started to bother her one day and she can't get this *meshuga'as* out of her head."

"I don't know how much I can accomplish in one hour, but I'll do the best I can."

When Bruriya entered my office, I was alarmed by her appearance. The tight muscles around her mouth caused it to assume a somber frown, which only accented the deep furrows in her brow. Her rounded back led me to believe that she was carrying a heavy burden on her shoulders. Distracted by the feeling of despondency she exuded, I nearly missed noticing the striking good looks she had been endowed with.

"Mazel tov! Have a seat, Bruriya," I said with a smile. I was not going to let her see that I was somewhat doubtful of being able to help her. "Make yourself comfortable. Can I offer you a glass of water?"

"No thank you. I just had a drink at home."

She spoke quickly, in a clipped sort of way, increasing my feeling that she was more tense than a tightly wound spring. I decided to skip the small talk and get right down into the meat of the issue. I had a box of tissues nearby and I wondered when she had smiled last.

"Your mother mentioned something about your having doubts. Can you tell me some more about that?"

"It's crazy and I can't explain it!" she said with emotion. "But one day I just started thinking that I made a mistake and my *chassan* is not for me. I'm scared to get married to him! It's so bad that I can't sleep at night!" She fought back the tears, so close to the surface and almost ready to flow.

I wanted to break her train of thought and give her a chance to un-wind somewhat. Mindful breathing was the quickest way to do that.

"Inhale and at the same time think to yourself the sound *'re,'*" I in-structed, "and then exhale as you think to yourself the sound *'laaaax.'* Make your out-breath long, even twice as long, as your in-breath."

I moved my hand upward as she inhaled and downward as she exhaled.

"Good. Repeat this breath five more times as you think to yourself *re-laaaax.*" The slow movement of my hand entrained her to breathe slowly and rhythmically. When she finished, she appeared decidedly more relaxed.

"Excellent! This is a very simple way for you to feel calmer. I'd like to speak to you when you are able to think logically and not carried away by emotion. Does this make sense?"

She nodded.

"Good. Anytime you feel yourself overcome with emotion please stop and do this *'re-laaaax'* breathing, even if you are in the middle of a sentence."

"OK."

"Great. I'd like to ask you a few questions. First of all, what is your *chassan*'s name?"

"Elimelech Heineman. His name really fits because he does have something majestic about him, something aristocratic."

"That's good to know. What is it about him that you like; that made you decide to marry him?"

"He's smart but he's also sensitive. He can relate to the other per-son and hear them out, and he can talk about things objectively. He has a sense of humor, learns well, and is well liked by his friends and by the *rebbeim* and the *mashgiach* in yeshiva. He's generous, because when his younger brother got engaged before him, he showered him with blessings and was really happy for him. That's what people told us. And he seems to be generous in many different ways."

"So, what is it about him that you don't like?"

"I don't know. He seems a lot smarter than me. Maybe he won't be happy with someone whose IQ is way less than his. Maybe I won't be able to talk to him on his level."

"Did he ever show you that in the time you spent together?"

"No, never. But maybe it's because he's being extra careful to be nice now. And then afterward, he'll have less tolerance for me than he did before."

"How long have you known him for?"

"About four months."

"And in that time did he ever treat you with disrespect or give you a feeling that he was looking down on you?"

"No. I never got that feeling."

"Did you ever see anything negative about him or hear any negative reports that would make you hesitate to marry him?"

"No, nothing! I can't think of anything. No one ever said a bad word about him."

"Did he do or say anything to make you begin doubting that he was the person he appeared to be? Anything that made you think that he was acting and covering up his true personality?"

"No! That's the crazy thing about this. There is nothing that I can think of to make me doubt him. But the doubts came anyway!"

"Do you want to break your engagement to Elimelech?" I asked quite bluntly.

"Not at all! I think he's a great person. I wish I could get rid of my unfounded fears, but I can't!" She was close to tears again.

"Is there anything about men in general that makes you feel unsure of their intentions, or makes you feel unsafe?"

"Nothing ever happened to me or to any friends of mine to make me nervous around men. Sure, I heard stories, but they never affected me personally."

I had to accept her words as true, for I was not about to dig into her past and look for problems. If she said nothing happened, I would take that as her reality.

"So, it seems we have a case of the *yetzer hara* doing his thing, trying to spoil something special, trying to mess up a good situation and turn it into a bad one! The *yetzer hara* is so crafty, he always seems to know a person's weak spots."

She suddenly started doing her "*re-laaaax*" breathing as I had taught her. It seems I had said something that touched a raw spot. When she stopped I gave her a glass of water. She took a few sips.

"Drinking water is good for flushing out bad feelings from your system. So keep your bottle of water with you."

"Now, let me ask you frankly. Do you think you are worthy of marrying such an aristocratic person that seems to have no faults?"

She hesitated before answering. "Actually, I'm not sure. I think he probably could do a better *shidduch* than me. But if Hashem sent him to me then I ought to be grateful and thankful."

"Is it possible that he sees qualities in you that you don't see in yourself? If he's so smart, could it be that he's more discerning than you are? Could it be that he sees things in you that are complementary to his character and personality, things that you don't see as positive traits, but that he sees as exactly what's missing in his life? Maybe he doesn't need someone as smart as he is, but yearns for someone who can give him support in other ways. Is that possible?"

She had to admit that it was possible.

"Is it possible that in general you do not recognize the good, the positive, the exemplary in yourself? Could it be that in general you're always hard on yourself, critical of your faults, demanding more and more of yourself? Could that be?"

Again, she had to admit that it was possible that she had always been too hard on herself.

"Do you believe that Hashem runs the world and manipulates events in the way He deems best?"

"Of course I do! I'd be an *apikores* if I thought differently!" Bruriya seemed offended by my question.

I continued to dig into her *hashkafic* beliefs and outlook on life. "Do you believe that *shidduchim* are made in Heaven and that Hashem manipulates happenings to bring them about?"

She was less heated as she answered this time. "Yes, I do. However, we know of situations where mistakes were made and the match had to be broken, either before or after the marriage took place."

"Yes, indeed," I agreed with her. "When one discovers a good reason, or at the very least, has a strong doubt about the integrity of the other party, the match could, and maybe even should, be broken. But in the absence of a good reason, what would be the justification to do that? If it was a match made in Heaven, why would one doubt the appropriateness, no, the goodness, of it?"

"I hear what you're saying and agree with you. But that's why my crazy feelings of doubt are so frustrating!"

"As I said before, your crazy feelings of doubt are simply the *yetzer hara*'s way of upsetting you, because when you feel so down you cannot serve Hashem properly. The *yetzer hara* has cleverly used your own low self-esteem to get you to doubt Hashem's goodness and wisdom in putting the two of you together. Trusting a little more in Hashem's plan for your life would easily get rid of your 'crazy feelings.' Does this make sense?"

"It makes sense, but the *yetzer hara* has caught me in his grip and I can't shake him loose! I tried drilling into myself all the right ideas of *emunah* and *bitachon* in Hashem's wisdom, but it didn't work. My parents did that with me too, but I still can't shake the feeling!"

I decided to try another tactic. "Did you ever hear the expression, 'a paper tiger'?"

"No. What does it mean?"

"The Chinese have festivals in which people parade around with animals made of paper such as tigers and dragons. They move them about on poles, making them appear very frightening. But since they are lifeless, made of rice paper or paper-mâché, despite their scary facade, they are powerless. There is an expression in the world today, 'He's a paper tiger,' which means that a person, a nation, or an institution that seems to pose a threat is actually ineffective or powerless."

Her eyes opened wide, as she was drawn into the spell of learning things completely foreign to her.

"But how can you get rid of a paper tiger?" she wanted to know, expressing her lingering doubt over the ability of the paper tiger to harm her.

"Simple. You strike a match and hold it up against the tiger and poof, it's gone!"

"But in real life..."

"You know, Bruriya, we could talk from today till tomorrow and not resolve anything. The best way I know of to achieve change is to engage your subconscious mind. That's the way I work. That's the way I get results."

"So what should we do?"

"With your permission, allow me to guide you into a deep state of relaxation. In this state your mind will be open to suggestion. The suggestions I hope to implant into your subconscious mind will enable you to overcome this challenge. Sounds good?"

"It sounds wonderful. Let's give it a shot."

She appeared calmer simply by hearing that I believed I had a solution. Of course, I had no idea if I would come up with a solution, but I always tried my best to instill a sense of confidence that with Hashem's help it would happen.

"Make yourself comfortable in the chair..." I intoned.

I spent a long time doing the induction, bringing her into a deep trance state, as she was obviously extremely tense. When I felt she was ready, I began the therapy.

"Enjoy the feeling of relaxation...of letting go...of being at peace...of being taken care of.... You know that you are not alone...that you are here in this world...with Hashem.... Hashem watches over you...loves you...protects you...guides you...in just the right way.... Hashem holds you close...just like a loving mother...holding her baby...providing for it...exactly what it needs.... Like David HaMelech said, 'K'gamul alei imo—Like a nursling in its mother's arms'...Hashem has a plan for you...and in His great love for you...will make that plan...unfold...in just the right way.... Feel now the warmth of Hashem's love for you...as He holds and protects you...like a baby in her mother's arms.... Let me know when you feel that...by a small nod of your head...."

I waited for her nod which took a bit of time in coming.

"You are so special...one of a kind....There is no other person...in this world...that is just like you.... You are a child of Hashem...a princess...a beautiful and special princess.... You are unique...and Hashem has given you a unique mission to fulfill.... Hashem needs you to fulfill this mission...and that is why He gives you life...so that you can fulfill your mission during your lifetime.... If your mission were fulfilled...you would no longer need to remain here...in this world.... And since you woke up this morning...you know you still...need to fulfill your very special...unique mission.... That's why you are here...and Hashem is going to help you...accomplish your mission in life...."

I paused, giving her time to absorb the message.

"Your mission is so special...one of a kind...so unique...that the *yetzer hara*...is doing his best...to get you to abort the mission....He is working overtime...to get you to stop...trying to fulfill your mission...because that mission is so very special...so important.... He wouldn't be trying so hard...to stop you...if it wasn't such an important mission.... But since he is trying so hard...you know it is a most important...and special mission....

"You realize that if this mission is so important...and Hashem desires that you fulfill it...you have the ability to fulfill it...no matter what strategies...the *yetzer hara* uses on you...no matter what tricks he plays on you....

"The *yetzer hara* has taken your wish...to build a *bayis ne'eman b'Yisrael*...a true and loyal Jewish home...dedicated to fulfilling Hashem's will...and turned it into something else....The *yetzer hara* has managed to turn it into fear...of doing what you wish to do...to create a beautiful Torah true home...with your very special...very aristocratic...very smart...very kind and sensitive prince...your *chassan*...your Elimelech...the perfect partner for your very special and unique purpose...in this world....

"I'd like you to see him now...your Elimelech...the perfect partner... for your special mission.... See him now...kind and sensitive...generous...caring...listening...supporting...being your perfect partner... in building your *bayis ne'eman b'Yisrael*....See him now...supporting you in so many ways...in just the right way.... See your beautiful...special Torah-true home...with you and him together...a prince and princess...creating your royal home...for Hashem...together...."

I gave her a fair amount of time to visualize. I noticed her expression soften as a gentle smile graced her lips.

"That crafty *yetzer hara* acts as though...he is stronger than you.... He makes believe that he is invincible.... But you have...exactly what you need...to overcome him.... He has taken your beautiful desire of creating a *bayis ne'eman b'Yisrael*...and turned it into something ugly...something deformed.... It looks like a ferocious tiger...a dangerous scary tiger....

"You felt afraid of it...in the *past*...before you knew the truth...that this is really only a paper tiger.... In the *past*...you thought it was a real tiger...a tiger that could destroy you.... In the *past* you were afraid of it.... But *now* you know the truth...that it only appears dangerous...scary...ferocious.... But it is really just made of paper....

"Paper cannot harm you...it has no power...it is just an illusion...without any ability...to do anything to you.... In the *past*, it made you afraid.... But *now* that you know it is only paper...you are happy...because you *now* know exactly what to do...to get rid of it...to make it disappear...and leave you in peace.... You are happy because *now* there is such a simple solution.... You are not afraid of paper.... You are stronger than paper.... And all the tricks of the *yetzer hara*...cannot give that tiger any power.... You are so happy that the solution is here...***now***...such a simple solution....

"You *now* take out a little wooden match...and you *now* strike the match head...and watch *now* as it ignites...and burns with a bright flame.... And you *now* approach fearlessly...that scary-looking tiger...and you *now* thrust the match into its belly.... And you step back and watch *now* as the flame...easily...effortlessly consumes the paper tiger...until it is no more.... It is gone.... You *now* are free...of the paper tiger...and the *yetzer hara*...cannot make you afraid again...because you *now* know the truth...."

I paused twice as long as I had previously, before speaking of the happy future. I described the yet-to-happen future events in the present tense, so that her mind would take in the scene as something that was literally taking place right then, as though it were fact and not visualization.

"And you see yourself...sitting in the *kallah* chair...on the day of your wedding...with such joy in your heart...because you overcame the paper tiger...and the tricks of the *yetzer hara*...and you know that you...are fulfilling your mission.... Perhaps this is only one part of your mission...but such an important part...because Hashem helped you....And He gave you the ability to do that...to destroy the paper tiger...that threatened you.... But you are stronger...and you overcame...and you are *now*...happy and excited...to create a beautiful life together...with your prince...your perfect partner.... See him approaching you...for the *badeken*...before your *chuppah*...with such a joyous expression on his face....And you smile in joy and excitement...in anticipation of the wonderful life...you will create together.... See that wonderful life...together in your beautiful home.... And know...that this is meant to be...."

I paused for several minutes, allowing the message to engrave itself into her subconscious mind, as I studied her face closely. Her brow was now smooth as tempered glass. Her cheek muscles had relaxed, soft as rose petals, allowing her lips to form a sweet smile. Her expression was one of total tranquility, which led me to believe that we had accomplished the goal. But I would not know for sure until speaking to her.

I brought her out of hypnosis and she stretched and yawned before looking at me. She was still partially in trance, and I used the opportunity to reinforce my suggestions.

"How do you feel now that you have vanquished the tiger?"

"I feel great! It seems too good to be true! I'm just wondering, does this great feeling actually last?"

I spoke slowly, using my hypnotic tone of voice. "*B'ezras Hashem*, of course it will last. I want you to say this affirmation numerous times a day, 'I feel great and know that I will never go back to fearing a paper tiger'.... You cannot go back to a place of falsehood once you know the truth. Right?"

"It's that simple?"

I responded by using a more emphatic tone of voice. "Yes, it is that simple. You are in control *now*, and can control your doubts and emotions. Right?"

"Right! I do feel it," she said excitedly. "Yes, I know that I can!"

"Wonderful!" I could feel her sincerity and knew she wasn't faking her response. "I want you to practice the '*re-laaaax*' breathing exercise I taught you for ten minutes twice a day. You can also do it in bed before dropping off to sleep. This will allow you to release any accumulated tension and help you to sleep soundly. And say your affirmation often, whenever you remember."

"Sure. I absolutely will! That's a small task to fulfill in exchange for peace of mind!"

"You should have an amazing wedding and a wonderful life together!"

"Please come!" Bruriya said as she handed me a wedding invitation. "You'll be a most honored guest."

"I can't promise, but I'll try my best."

We hugged and she left.

I was not able to attend the wedding, but her mother gave me a full report. Bruriya was a happy and radiant bride. Her paper tiger remained dust and ashes.

6

INFERTILITY

Shoshana Roth

Shoshana was married for fifteen years and had never been blessed with the gift of motherhood. Her doctors were unable to discover the cause of the couple's infertility as the tests they ran were in the normal range. Despite the numerous treatments she underwent, modern medicine was not able to achieve the desired goal. The doctors had given up on trying to give Shoshana and her husband their longed-for child and suggested they begin adoption procedures.

Shoshana was very depressed, and a friend of hers thought I might be able to help. Although she did not have much faith in hypnosis, Shoshana felt she had to give any legitimate healing modality a chance at enabling her to become a mother, and so reluctantly set up an appointment with me.

In our first session Shoshana expressed a lot of her pain and frustration. She also had a fair amount of anger at some of her doctors who had treated her as a "case" and totally lacked sensitivity toward her feelings.

It was good for Shoshana to let out the pressures building up inside, but I wanted to learn more about her, her life and her past. For one thing, I was pleased that she was happily married and was able to express herself openly to her husband. However, her childhood was something else entirely.

Her parents had endured a very rocky marriage. Shoshana's mother would talk to her daughter as though she were a friend, with whom she shared her woes. She vehemently expressed her angry feelings toward her spouse in their conversations together. One shocking statement haunted Shoshana, when her mother admitted to feelings of regret over having children. Had she not been obligated to care for them, she would have then felt free to leave her husband.

Shoshana would try to calm her mother down, make her feel better and do her best to smooth things out between her parents. Not only would the child often find herself in the position of mothering her mother, but she was also given the job of caring for her younger brother as though she actually were his mother. Shoshana was required to be home for her brother as her mother came home late from work. She also had to make meals for the family and clean up afterward.

At the point when her parents finally divorced, her mother broke down emotionally and could no longer work. Shoshana left school and took a job in order to hold the family together. Her mother deteriorated to the point where she developed Alzheimer's at a relatively young age. She was so ill that she was unable to take her daughter to the *chuppah* and an aunt and uncle replaced her parents on that special day in her life.

She claimed that she didn't blame her mother for her inability to nurture her, yet she could not erase the deep bitterness caused by her dysfunctional upbringing. Her mother had died years earlier, and so she was unable to talk to her about her feelings. At least with me she could.

Shoshana expressed that she had never had a childhood. She had been thrust into the position of "mother" as far back as she could remember. And it had not been a happy position. Consciously, Shoshana wanted to be a mother; subconsciously, she felt a loathing toward that role.

I could clearly see that "motherhood" was not a beautiful or cherished concept in Shoshana's perception. For her, it could only bring feelings of discomfort, pain, frustration, anger, remorse, and who knew what else. I had to make her realize that the past was the past and could remain in the past, and her present life could be entirely different.

I wondered if Shoshana had ever seen a model of motherhood that appealed to her. I wanted to discover whether there was anyone in her life about whom she could say that she was a wonderful mother. Did she even know what a loving, nurturing mother was? As motherhood had its negative associations for her, my task would be to make Shoshana understand that there were other ways of perceiving that exalted vocation.

The first thing we did together in hypnosis was for my client to recognize how emotionally compromised her mother had been when Shoshana was growing up and how she had been incapable of acting differently. I took her back in time to her childhood, to those difficult years when she was obliged to fill the role of "mother."

"See yourself now...in the kitchen making supper...for the family.... You are tired but you know that your mother is even more tired.... She works so hard...and comes home so late...and has no emotional support from your father.... She is very unhappy in her life.... Do you know how unhappy she is?.... She wants to rest...but she cannot.... She must bring home the money...to provide for her two young children.... She has no strength...to give you the love you deserve...to take care of you...as a mother does.... She wants to love you...and take care of you...but she does not have the strength.... By now she has forgotten how to be a mother...to her sweet children.... Can you feel her pain?.... She wants to mother you...but she does not know how to.... She is crying inside...because she wants to love you...and does not remember how.... She has even forgotten how to say thank you to you...for making supper...because she is so tired...and so sad....

"You hear her at the front door.... She walks into the kitchen...and drops into a chair...not able to smile at you...because she is so tired...and so sad.... She wants to smile at you and to love you...you and your brother...but she has forgotten how.... What do you feel in your heart...for this unfortunate lady...that is your mother?"

It took Shoshana several moments before she answered. "I feel sorry for her...for my mother.... I am not angry anymore...that I have to make supper...and clean up.... I feel so sorry for her."

I continued reframing the situation for Shoshana until she came to the point where she realized that her mother had never meant to cause her daughter harm but was simply incapable of doing any better in her mothering. She realized that now that her mother was in the world of truth, she was surely very sorry for any damage she had inflicted upon her child.

"Shoshana," I continued, "tell your mother what you feel for her.... Imagine that she is here now...and let her know what you told me....Make her feel better...by letting her know how you feel now...about all those years growing up at home.... Tell her now."

"Mommy...it's OK," she said haltingly. "I know you wanted to love me...and you did not know how...you forgot how.... It's OK, I'm not angry.... I love you.... I forgive you...with all my heart...."

She began crying. I believed they were cleansing tears, as she began releasing old pent-up emotions, stored up over many long years.

"I know you never wanted...to hurt me in any way...but just did not know how to be different.... When you broke down...got dementia...I really understood that you couldn't be different.... But now I understand even more....I can let go of all the bad feelings...and only love you...and wish you good in the *olam ha'emes*."

That was an excellent beginning for Shoshana's healing; letting go of anger, resentment, and pain. The next step of our journey would be to discover some positive relationships she had had with women who also happened to be mothers.

By digging into Shoshana's past, I discovered that she had experienced some wonderful times together with several women in her life; an aunt, a friend's mother, and her own grandmother. I used these experiences as examples of how these women, who themselves were mothers, were able to love and nurture others. While in trance, I had her absorb the positive qualities of these women into her own being as she interacted with them. She experienced herself helping them care for their children in loving ways.

While in hypnosis I then moved her through different scenarios in which she saw herself caring for other women's children of all ages, as a babysitter, yet doing so lovingly, as though they were her own children.

"You are watching your neighbor's baby...a cute six-month-old baby girl.... She cries and you pick her up.... You hold her in your arms...and rock her.... She feels so soft...she smells so sweet...she is so warm.... You hold her against your body...very carefully...and lovingly...rocking her lovingly...until she stops crying.... You smile at her and make cooing sounds...and she smiles at you.... She is so precious.... You know that Hashem has such a sweet baby...for you too.... You can be curious to know...when He will send her to you.... But right now, you take care of...your neighbor's baby...very carefully...and lovingly...as if she were your own."

Shoshana confirmed for me that she felt confident in caring for the children she was visualizing. She let me know that she felt increased joy each time she was put into that nurturing role.

When I believed she was ready for the next step I had her imagine herself pregnant and sending loving thoughts to her unborn baby.

"As you send those loving thoughts to your baby...can you feel something coming back to you?....

"What you give out...comes back...that's the way Hashem set up the world[ii].... You send out love...and then feel how...it comes back to you...and then send it out again...and have this love go round and round...round and round...in loving circles."

I had Shoshana confirm with each step along the road to healing that she felt the positive feelings I was bringing up. She expressed her longing to hold her baby in her arms, cradling and caring for it.

The next step was for Shoshana to see herself as a mother, caring, loving, nurturing, and reveling in the role of motherhood. This step was quite easily accomplished as much of the work of changing her previous perceptions had already been done.

It was most important for Shoshana to eliminate any negative thinking concerning her ability to conceive a baby. Lack of belief in her body's ability to conceive and bring a pregnancy to a successful conclusion could undermine the work we had done up to this point.

"Here is a list of twenty different affirmations," I said as I handed her a sheet of paper. "These are positive statements about pregnancy, birth, and mothering. I want you to pick two statements from each category and say them, preferably out loud, at least three times a day. You can make up your own affirmations if you wish. The best way is to say them to yourself in front of the mirror, being sure to smile as you say the words.

"The more you believe that Hashem will enable you to become a mother, the more you do your part to make it happen. Just in case Hashem decides otherwise, you will accept His decision with courage, knowing that Hashem knows what is best for you. But at the same time as knowing that the outcome is totally up to Hashem, we do significant *hishtadlus* to make our desires come true. And a very important way is first by believing that Hashem will make it happen, and second by imagining as vividly as you can that it is actually happening. I'll prepare an audio recording for you to make it easier for you to visualize your dream coming true. You'll want to listen to it every day."

I then taught her breathing exercises to keep her relaxed and lower her cortisol levels. Elevated cortisol, a stress hormone, could easily interfere with her reproductive hormones.

If Shoshana had previously thought there was not much more that she could do to actualize her dream of becoming a mother, she now knew how mistaken she had been. I had followed the words of Yirmiyahu HaNavi (4:3), "*Niru lachem nir v'al tizre'u el kotzim*—Break up for you a fallow ground, and sow not among thorns." We had prepared the ground of her "garden" by removing the thorns, stones, and bugs, the negative feelings and perceptions, and replacing them with freshly turned earth, her new positive perceptions. Then we "fertilized" her garden plot with plenty of oxygen, relaxation techniques, and positive visualizations. She had obtained a full toolbox of techniques to use in her quest. And use them she did, as she conscientiously said her fertility affirmations, practiced her breathing exercises, and listened to the visualization recording consistently.

Her "garden" was primed and ready to receive the seeds of growth, and Hashem responded to her efforts. Within a few months of our beginning work together, Shoshana was expecting her baby. Our joy was boundless upon the birth of her healthy little girl.

Shaindel Levine

Shaindel insisted on coming to me for sessions although I had great doubts of being able to help her. She had been married for over thirty years, from the tender age of seventeen, and had still not been blessed with a child. She had undergone fertility treatments for years, suffering numerous failed in vitro fertilization (IVF) procedures. I told her that hypnosis was not magic, but she rebutted my argument by saying, "This is my last chance. My doctor said he's going to try only one more time! Please, please, try to help me!"

I obviously could not refuse such a heartfelt plea. I agreed to take her on as a client if she promised to faithfully practice the exercises I gave her. If not, I felt there was no point in her spending her precious time, money, and effort with halfhearted motivation. I wanted a strong commitment of compliance before we began. She agreed to my terms.

From the medical point of view, Shaindel's doctors had clearly defined her problem and were doing all that modern medicine could offer. Statistically, their strategies should have worked. But they didn't. I had to assume that there was an underlying emotional cause for why her body wasn't responding as one would have expected it to.

I also wanted to discover more about her personality before forming a plan for healing.

"Tell me, Shaindel, when was the last time you underwent an IVF procedure?"

"Over a year ago. My doctor wanted me to rest up from all the stress it involves before trying one last time."

"How do you feel when going through the procedure?"

"Awful! I'm so nervous that I can't sleep, my blood pressure shoots up as well as my sugar levels. I have to go on diabetic medication because my sugar gets totally out of control."

"Do you suffer with high levels of sugar at other times?" I wanted to know.

"Maybe a little bit. The doctor says it's because I'm so full of stress. He also threatened to put me on blood-pressure medicine. I'm taking so many pills that I don't care if he gives me one more. But I'd like it if I could manage my stress better and have my blood pressure normalize on its own."

Despite her age, rapidly approaching fifty years, her face was youthful. Her large brown eyes clearly expressed her despair. I strained to hear the barely audible words, as her hunched posture muffled the sounds. She dabbed at her eyes repeatedly with the crumpled tissue she clutched.

"I imagine that those few weeks are the most stressful in a woman's life," I said, "and probably for her husband too."

"My husband runs away to the Kosel or to Rashbi's *kever* to daven. He can't bear to see me agonizing over whether the procedure will succeed or fail. It's painful for him too, but he doesn't say a word. I also don't talk to anybody at this time, because I'm too emotional. I don't want to upset my mother-in-law and I don't have a mother. I don't even have a sister I feel comfortable speaking to. So I suffer on my own until the waiting period passes. Once the IVF fails, I almost feel better, because the tension of not knowing ends."

Her words shot forth with a rush, and I wondered if this was the first time she was expressing these emotions to anyone.

"Thank you for sharing," I said, with empathy. "I can certainly understand why you feel so stressed. But let's start with the basics. Stress can be very detrimental to the working of our bodies. It can affect our hormones, which are especially sensitive, and can cause them to respond negatively under its influence."

"What do you mean? When I'm stressed, it's just a feeling I'm feeling. How can it affect my hormones?" Her puzzled expression was an improvement over the sadness I had seen just moments before. She was in an open and receptive state, ready to learn things she never knew before.

"The stress you feel is more than just a feeling," I said. "It causes your glands to release stress hormones, such as adrenalin and cortisol. When our body is flooded with these hormones, more than is healthy for us, they can affect us negatively. Medical studies show that stress can disrupt the metabolism, which means you may have trouble sleeping, your digestion suffers, you can feel depressed and irritable, and it can even cause an outbreak of acne.

"In relation to fertility, elevated levels of cortisol can affect the hypothalamus, the part of your brain that regulates hormones. It can inhibit the body's main reproductive hormone, GnRH, which regulates your cycle. That could mean you ovulate later than usual, or not at all. It might even cause a woman to stop menstruating. One infertility researcher, Dr. Alice Domar,[iii] says that your body is smart. It knows that when you are undergoing stress it's not a good time to have a baby.

"It's quite a common occurrence for a girl, before she gets married, to have her cycle go completely haywire because of her stress. Do you know of such cases?"

"Yes, sure. It happened to a few of my friends."

"I actually worked with several clients who suffered with hormonal imbalances for years. After doing hypnotherapy for a while, we were able to get things back to normal."

"Really? I understand what you're saying. But the doctors are giving me my hormones artificially. So why don't they work as they should?"

"A person is more complicated than one plus one equals two. There are lots of things going on that can affect the way our body responds. Let's just say that in my experience I have found that when someone learns how to relax effectively, many significant changes can take place. We don't always have to understand how. We trust that Hashem is helping us achieve our desired goals when we do things at a deeper level, at a soul level. I have seen things happen that don't make sense in the laboratory, but they do when we understand the mind-body connection. And without Hashem enabling these techniques to work, they won't. I hope you agree that what we are doing here is a form of *hishtadlus* that doctors don't know much about but that we must not ignore."

"So what should I do?" she asked plaintively.

"The first and most basic thing is to learn deep breathing and some other relaxation techniques. This will help you enormously in many areas of your life. Your blood pressure may come down. Your sugar levels too. I'm certainly not promising anything, but it might happen. And I'm convinced that you'll be able to sleep better with regular practice.

"You will be preparing your body for the next attempt at IVF. It's like preparing a garden. If you want a productive garden then before you plant anything you will first remove the stones, dig up the weeds, turn the earth, get rid of the bugs, put in fertilizer, and only then plant the seeds or plants. If you don't do that, many of your seedlings won't grow; they will perish because the ground is not nurturing them. So what we are doing now is preparing your garden for planting, removing the different things that can prevent growth, and adding the things that encourage growth. Then we have a much better chance of reaping a good crop. Does this make sense?"

After a moment of contemplation Shaindel straightened her hunched posture, and looked at me straight in the eye. "Yes, it does," she said. "That's why I came to you. I knew I needed this kind of work and needed a professional that could get me to relax. I know that because what I tried in the past didn't help enough."

"What did you try in the past?"

"Of course, I read *Tehillim* every day, as I have since I was a young girl. I love saying *Tehillim*, but I still felt anxious. I said *Perek Shirah* for forty days, but it didn't seem to do anything for me. I listened to recordings of many different rabbis who promised all kinds of *yeshuos*. They gave me hope but nothing happened. I tried different *segulos*, I drank special potions, I got *berachos* from *mekubalim*, I fasted. Maybe there were more things I did; I can't remember. I felt relaxed or at peace only immediately after doing any of that, but never for an extended period of time. I'm probably missing a lot of *emunah* and *bitachon* in Hashem."

"Please don't be hard on yourself," I said encouragingly. "Everything you did surely gave you merit, because you tried to attain greater levels of *emunah* and peace of mind. But maybe the time for your *yeshuah* still hadn't come. I'll teach you a new type of *hishtadlus* and we will daven that Hashem accepts it to help you attain your goal of motherhood. Always put your trust in Hashem, while at the same time put forth serious effort to help yourself. It is a most desirable trait to be relaxed and happy. It can only help you in life and in being a better servant of Hashem, and *b'ezras Hashem* in becoming a mother!"

"Do you think we will succeed?" she asked in a whisper.

"I don't know. I'm not a *navi*, I can't tell the future. We will do, to the best of our ability, the things that seem important to do, and pray that Hashem grants you your wish."

I spent the rest of the session teaching her deep breathing exercises and techniques for relaxing the vagus nerve, a large nerve in the body that affects many bodily functions, including reproductive endocrine disorders. I also had her visualize a happy memory that made her feel good to the degree that it brought a smile to her lips. When experiencing this type of memory, her body was being flooded with "happy hormones" such as endorphins, serotonin, melatonin, dopamine, and oxytocin. The effect of the happy hormones on her systems would be proven over time. Additionally, they might undo the damage the stress hormones had wrought in her body.

I then taught her the anchor technique. The anchor would be attached to the feelings the happy memory generated and allowed her to feel them instantly. She could activate her anchor any time she felt stressed, sad, or lonely. She could do it in the doctor's waiting room, in his office while going through examinations or procedures, and at home while waiting to hear the lab results. I told her to practice her exercises at least three times a day, but the more often she did, the better and faster results she would see.

I explained that these exercises were foundational and were precursors to the hypnosis I planned on doing. Through hypnosis I could find the specific "bugs" in her garden that we needed to be rid of.

Shaindel appeared much brighter at her next appointment. She had practiced the exercises faithfully and was eager to begin the "inner work." She was an excellent hypnotic subject, reaching deep states of trance easily and effortlessly.

During the weeks I worked with Shaindel, I discovered many reasons for her feeling stupid, inadequate, unworthy, and even that she was being punished. We dealt with each episode she brought up from her subconscious mind and successfully neutralized those feeling through various hypnotherapy visualizations and techniques. The work felt like peeling the layers off of an onion, for when we dealt successfully with one negative perception, another one would appear.

And then one day while in hypnosis, she expressed a belief that she had been cursed and that was at the root of her problem. This was a most challenging perception to undo and I considered this episode as being traumatic for Shaindel. Whether or not it actually was the reason for her infertility was not as much of an issue as the fact that she believed it was. If in her mind the "curse" was preventing her from conceiving, she might, unknowingly, be sabotaging her own success. I needed to undo her belief that this curse was getting in the way of her dream coming true. Once I did that, her physiology would change, since the mind affects the body for the good or the bad, and then her body would be able to respond to the medical interventions positively.

"Please tell me what happened," I said while she was still in trance. "Tell me all the details of when and why you were being cursed.... The more I know, the easier it will be for me to help you."

She began her tale quietly, speaking slowly. "My mother always encouraged me to do *chessed* with old people.... I was fifteen years old and there was this old *almanah*...Tante Fraidel...I did shopping for her...cleaned her house.... She wanted me to sit and talk to her.... I did three or four times a week.... We became friends...even though she wasn't completely normal.... When I was seventeen years old, I became engaged.... She told me that I must daven for her...under my *chuppah*...that she should be healthy and live long.... She wanted my *tefillah*...specifically when I was standing under the *chuppah*.... She made me promise...and I promised....

"Under my *chuppah*...I mentally prayed for her.... Afterward...when I told her what I had done...she screamed, 'You only thought the *tefillah*...and didn't say the words with your mouth?.... How could you do that?!.... You promised me that you would daven!.... Daven means you say the words...not just think them!'

"She didn't listen to me...telling her that I misunderstood...that I really wanted to daven for her.... She was so angry...that she cursed me...saying that I should never enjoy my marriage...never have children.... She refused to accept my apologies...even though I begged her many times.... And she never wanted me...to come to her ever again."

Shaindel sat silent and despondent. I could easily see why she believed this episode to be at the root of her problem. Although this incident hadn't come up immediately at the start of our work, as she might have been suppressing the memory of it in the recesses of her mind, under hypnosis it had finally surfaced. This was a very important piece of the puzzle and I thanked Hashem for this revelation.

"Shaindel, I'd like to thank your subconscious mind...for giving us this important bit of information.... When was the last time you asked Tante Fraidel for forgiveness?"

"Maybe...twenty-nine years ago.... She died a short time after it happened."

"I see.... When was the last time you thought of her?"

"Not for many years.... I forgot about her.... I only remembered now...."

"Good!.... That means your subconscious mind...is telling us to pay attention to this story.... You need to think about her again...to realize something.... Is it not possible that she changed her mind...and no longer wishes you ill?"

"How can we know that? She's dead...."

"Her body is no more...but she lives on in the spiritual world.... Her *neshamah* exists.... After all the good deeds you did for her...and after all of your suffering...for so many years...I'm sure she will only want...good and happiness for you.... In the world of truth...she will never want to bear a grudge against you.... She will understand that you misunderstood her...that you really wanted to daven...for her well-being...that you were a good girl.... In the world of truth, she can't possibly want to hurt or harm you.... She will only want to forgive you...."

Shaindel sat quietly, nodding her head in agreement. I could see she was ready for the next crucial step, for her to feel in her heart, and not just know in her intellect, that she was truly forgiven.

"It's really very simple..." I said with a voice full of conviction. "Tante Fraidel's *neshamah* exists....I'm sure she would only want to help you...if she possibly could.... You understand that as well as I...but now you will, *b'siyata d'Shmaya*, feel just how true this is....

"I'd like you to go deeper now...deeper and deeper...into that place...where you can see things...and hear things...that you cannot see and hear...normally...."

I spent some time inducing a deeper trance state. When I felt she was ready, I continued the therapy.

"In a moment...I'm going to ask you to imagine Tante Fraidel coming...coming to you here...and you can imagine...what you would say to her...if you could meet her again."

The reader should, in no way, understand this to mean that, *chas v'shalom*, I was acting as a medium and performing some "hocus-pocus" to bring the soul of the deceased to interact with us. Doing that is completely forbidden. I merely wanted Shaindel to imagine that she was talking to the *neshamah* of the *niftar* in whichever way she would visualize her. This would give her the opportunity to ask for forgiveness once again.

Although intellectually she may have understood that she had already been forgiven, it seemed to me that deep down, she was not convinced. Her guilt feelings may have created internal blocks strong enough to obstruct a pregnancy. By my placing her in the scenario of asking and receiving forgiveness in her imagination, I wanted her to experience that truth so vividly in her inner being that it would become her new reality. Once she could truly feel forgiven, her body would respond in kind.

The hypnotic subject imagines what her subconscious mind truly wants to see happening in her life. And, therefore, it was not far-fetched for me to believe that she would imagine that forgiveness was being granted to her. She would then feel immense relief as a result, which would affect her body positively, allow healing to take place, and *b'siyata d'Shmaya* remove any blockages that might have been preventing her from conceiving.

"Take a moment now...to imagine her coming here...appearing in your presence...and you will tell her what you told me...how much you wanted to daven for her well-being.... And then ask her forgiveness for making a silly mistake...because you did not understand her....Your *tefillah* was still a real *tefillah*...under the *chuppah*...accepted by Hashem.... But you need to know that she forgives you now....

"In a moment you will feel her presence here...and then I will wait quietly...while you ask for forgiveness.... Imagine her coming now.... Let me know...with a nod of your head...when you sense her here...in front of you...."

By letting Shaindel know I was quite sure that she would visualize Tante Fraidel next to her I gave her an indirect message that that is exactly what would happen. And if she believed it would happen, in most cases, it would. And so I waited for the head nod, which came fairly quickly, and remained quiet for a few minutes. I could see varied emotions crossing Shaindel's facial features as she interacted with her imaginary visitor. After an appropriate amount of time I continued speaking.

"Were you happy…to imagine meeting with Tante Fraidel?"

She nodded.

"Was Tante Fraidel happy…to meet with you?"

Again, she nodded.

"Did she accept your apology?"

Again, she nodded in the affirmative.

"Please tell me what she said to you."

She had a hard time forming the words, a sign she was still in a deep trance.

"She said…'I'm not angry…I love you…I give you…a thousand blessings…for Hashem to give you…a baby soon….'"

Shaindel was crying silently, tears of joy. I handed her a tissue.

"She was shining…so loving…she told me to be happy…not to worry anymore…."

"Shaindel, why don't you bless Tante Fraidel for her kindness," I said, "and tell her you will do good deeds for her *aliyas neshamah*."

After a short while, I slowly brought Shaindel out of hypnosis.

Shaindel stared at me with big round eyes. "That was unbelievable. It seemed as though she really was there. She was so kind, so generous, so loving. Just like a pure *neshamah* would be, different from how she was in life. A *neshamah* could only be forgiving, and never hold a grudge!"

"How did it feel when she forgave you?"

"Fantastic! She was so happy and eager to say the words."

"Let's think of her as a *shaliach* of Hashem! Now that you believe that she no longer bears a grudge against you for what you did in the past there might no longer be a reason to withhold your *yeshuah*." I paused, letting the implications of my words sink in.

"So continue to daven, to practice your relaxation techniques, and do many acts of kindness for the elevation of Tante Fraidel's *neshamah*. And wait with patience and happiness in your heart."

We continued meeting regularly in order to reinforce all that she had learned. She appeared a much happier and relaxed woman than the one I had met at our first meeting. Once she began the IVF procedure, the last one her doctor would perform on her, the relaxation exercises were more important than ever.

The two-week waiting period, a time in which success or failure hung in the balance, was a nerve-wracking time for her as well as for me. We did not meet personally, as she wished to avoid traveling at this time, but we spoke nearly every day. We did mini-sessions on the phone and she was able to keep her blood pressure and blood sugar from climbing to unhealthy levels.

The day the two weeks elapsed, the day she would get her lab results, found me more than a little anxious. I told myself repeatedly that it was only up to Hashem to give Shaindel a child. Hypnosis was merely a conduit for blessing to take place, if Hashem so decreed. I knew that I had succeeded in giving her a better quality of life by all the work that we had done together. And those benefits I could certainly rate as success. Whether or not she saw her dream of becoming a mother come true would be the cream on the cake.

This internal chatter filled my mind all day as I tried to calm my emotions until I would get the longed-for phone call from Shaindel. I decided not to call her, as it was up to her to share the test results with me if she so chose. The hours passed and I received no call from her. To me that was a sign that the results were not good, otherwise why would she hold back from sharing the good news with me?

It must have been 10:00 p.m. when the phone rang. My heartbeat accelerated as I picked up the receiver. "Hello."

"Bracha, it's Shaindel." Her voice was quiet, as it usually was. "I got my lab results today."

"Yes, I know. I was waiting to hear from you."

"I didn't call you earlier, because I went to the Kosel with my husband. We spent hours there, davening in gratitude!"

"What?" I exclaimed somewhat too loudly.

"Yes, the test was positive! I can't believe it. I simply can't believe it!"

"Baruch Hashem! Wonderful news, absolutely wonderful!" I couldn't hold back the tears.

"Thank you so much! You were such a good *shaliach*!"

"Baruch Hashem that I was able to help you!" I responded. "That's the reason I do this work, so that I can help people. There is no greater privilege for me than to help others. That's why we were put in this world! And thank you for putting your trust in me."

"You know, Bracha," she added suddenly, fearfully. "I'm still very anxious! I won't feel safe until I finish the first three months. What if something happens?"

I could understand her apprehension. It was important to complete the first trimester successfully and healthfully. We decided to continue relaxation sessions by phone for the time being in order to keep her anxiety at bay, as well as to help control her physical symptoms. I also felt it important to coach her in nutritious eating.

The call came nearly nine months later. She had given birth to a healthy baby boy. She recuperated well and was the picture of a happy and healthy mother, enjoying her offspring as any mother would.

The exhilarating joy I felt gave me a high for several weeks. How true are the words *"Asur l'hisya'eish*—Never lose hope!" With Hashem, the impossible becomes possible and the extraordinary becomes ordinary!

7

FORGIVENESS

Bella Rosen

Shaindel's experience, her apparent gift of forgiveness from someone who was no longer alive, could be dismissed by a skeptic by saying
that it was the result of an active imagination striving to obtain something it so desperately wanted. The doubter could simply declare that
my client imagined the whole thing and, in reality, it had no effect on
the outcome of her medical treatments. There was no way for us to
know that the forgiveness and blessing she seemingly received was
real or that it made any difference in what happened afterward.

In my mind, however, Shaindel's experience was a magnificent example of the power of forgiveness to affect, not only the emotions,
but the physical body of the forgiven. To me this was absolutely clear,
although there was no way that I could actually prove it to be so.

I tend not to be overly concerned with presenting proofs to my
clients for how or why mind-body healing works. I always tell them
that salvation comes from Hashem and we are merely doing our
hishtadlus as we are meant to, in order to access Hashem's blessing.
As long as Hashem gives my client a positive outcome, does it really
matter how it came about?

Not long after Shaindel's amazing tale, Bella came into my life. She had suffered from a rare form of intestinal cancer and was now in remission. Her doctors were pleased with the results of the chemotherapy treatments as they had caught the cancer in its early stages. But Bella was not happy and desperately wanted to improve the quality of her life. Besides using a number of alternative medical treatments, she wished to change her state of mind.

At our first session, Bella was very verbal about her woes. She began our conversation with the stark statement, "I know why I have cancer." She then proceeded to list all the things that were wrong in her life. She had relationship issues with a number of people, an estranged sister, a demanding boss, jealous colleagues at work, and some neighbors angry over the addition they had made to their house, although in *beis din* the *rabbanim* had given them full rights to proceed. The issue that bothered her the most, however, was with her father who had passed away several years earlier.

In conclusion she stated, "It's eating me up!"

I could only agree with her that her miserable life had contributed to the cancer that was eating her up.

"I'm so sorry to hear that you are going through all of that," I said softly. "I hear you saying that you wish to get the negative feelings out of your system. *B'ezras Hashem*, I'll give you tools to deal with your anger, resentment, and frustration. Then your relationship with others will change for the better. Life can be experienced through rose-colored glasses if you learn how to obtain them and how to use them. Over time, you will feel a measure of tranquility, which may well improve your physical health."

"Yes! That is what I want! I feel imprisoned by my feelings, which I can't break free of. I want to feel happy and at peace despite all the horrible things that are happening to me."

"That's a tall order, but no reason to stop us from taking on the challenge."

"Please, do whatever you can," Bella said pleadingly. "Even a small improvement will make a big difference in my life."

"We will start with your perceptions, changing the way you see life. Are you ready to do that?"

"What do you mean?" she wanted to know.

"You can see the people in your life as 'out to get you, to hurt you, to harm you' and then you hate them and feel full of anger toward them. On the other hand, you can see them as acting out on their own issues they have fallen victim to and in need of some of your compassion."

"That's a bit of a stretch for me, but I'm willing to do the work. I'm even willing to have two sessions a week, because I have no idea how much time I have left in this world!"

Bella was familiar with breathing and relaxation techniques and that made our work much easier. After setting up a daily regime of exercises for her, I started the hypnotherapy.

Over the following weeks we saw major positive shifts in her varied relationships. She could not believe how, by doing her own inner work, life on the outside could change so much.

"It's really simple," I explained. "When people are in a dance together, holding hands in one large circle, if one dancer changes direction or rhythm it affects the whole circle. You are not living in a vacuum, and the changes you make send ripples out to the others in your circle. The changes in them may not come instantly or to the degree you wish, but as long as you persevere in making your positive changes, eventually they will happen."

The analogy made sense to her and we continued our work, seeing greater and greater success over time. But there was something else bothering her that she hadn't told me about. One day it came out.

"I have a lot of pain because of my son." She was clearly distressed.

"You never mentioned him to me before," I said. "Would you like to tell me what's going on?"

"Rafi has been married for six years now, and in all that time has not spoken to me. He and his wife and three children live in the Galilee. From time to time, we see each other at family *simchahs*, but neither he nor his wife speaks to me."

"How sad! Do they speak to your husband and other children?"

"Yes, their only issue is with me."

She described a series of misunderstandings between her and Rafi that had caused increasing friction over the years, and I had my doubts if we could resolve this thorny issue.

"I have tried so many times to improve our relationship," she added. "I go out of my way to be helpful to them, but it never makes a difference."

"My motto is, 'Never say never!'" I said encouragingly. "You may have made a lot of difference in the way he feels about you, although he prefers not to show it at this time. And his wife is just following his lead."

"I don't believe there is something I can do that will change things," she lamented.

"Do you want to work on it?" I asked.

"Not really. I need to focus on the people I am interacting with on a daily basis and there is only so much I can spend my energy on."

"We'll put Rafi on the back burner for now. We can always get back to him when you feel ready to."

"That makes sense," she agreed. "But I must admit that I can't put my father on the back burner. The fact that he died while we were still angry at each other is really eating me up! I am so happy with the changes going on with the people we worked on, but terribly sad over how things ended between my Dad and me. The sadness is outweighing the happiness!"

She began crying and reached for a tissue. I said nothing and allowed her to sit with her emotions. After a few minutes, she continued speaking.

"The feeling of regret is so strong. That's what I mean by 'it's eating me up.' It's something I should have taken care of but because of my weakness I let it slide. And then it was too late. And the regret I feel is so overwhelming!"

She blew her nose and looked out the window, maybe imagining a time when things were better between them.

"It's not really too late, you know," I said quietly. "There are ways to ask forgiveness from people who have passed on."

"I asked for forgiveness at his *levayah*," she said as she returned her focus onto me, "and have gone to his *kever* many times to do the same."

"Did you speak to a *rav* about what to do?" I wanted to know.

"Yes, and I followed his instructions carefully. And halachically I probably did all that I should have done. But I just don't feel that the issue is resolved."

"I quite understand. You would have wanted to hear him say the words, 'I forgive you, my daughter!' And now you think that it will never be."

"That's it! Hearing his loving voice would have been all that I needed. But now it's too late!"

"Had I said to you, 'If your father knew how much you are suffering, for sure he would want to help you and let you know that he has already forgiven you!' would you believe me?"

"Theoretically I know that could be," she answered hesitantly, "but how could I possibly know for sure?"

"Would you like to tell him how sorry you are and hear his response?"

Her jaw dropped and she stared at me, speechless, for a full thirty seconds. "How could I do that?" she finally whispered.

"It's simple, really," I explained. "We know that his *neshamah* exists; we know that the spiritual world exists. If you imagined your father's *neshamah* appearing to you, you could tell him exactly what you would have wanted to tell him before he died. Although you said those words at his *kever*, by imagining this encounter you can gain so much more. If Hashem grants you this great opportunity it will happen. And if not, then it won't happen. The only way to find out is to try. Would you like to?"

"I'd like to, but I'm not sure if I feel ready to," was her somewhat ambivalent reply.

I knew what she meant. She needed a bit of time to assimilate the idea that she could literally hear her father's words of forgiveness by imagining she was interacting with him.

"You don't have to do anything you don't feel up to. Actually, if you attempted to visualize this meeting now and your subconscious was not ready, because you were not emotionally ready, it would block it from happening. But that's fine. If it doesn't happen today it can happen at a different time. You really risk nothing."

I was not going to encourage her in taking this step, as it was truly important that she feel ready. This was her journey and she needed to travel it at her own pace. I was acting as someone she had chosen to facilitate her journey, and certainly not as someone who wished to impose her own beliefs on what should be done.

Bella sat quietly ruminating, while I prayed to Hashem silently to give me the Divine assistance needed to help her in the best way possible.

When Bella next looked at me, she was smiling softly. "Yes," she said, "I do think I'd like to try. As you said, there is nothing to lose, since we can always try again if nothing happens today."

"Exactly so. I'm going to place a box of tissues right on your lap just in case you need them."

After doing that I asked, "Are you ready?"

"Yes. I'm ready."

"Tell me, where was a place your father liked to be outside of his home?"

"He loved the seaside. Whenever he took vacation, with the family or alone, that's where he would go."

"Nice! There's one other thing I want you to do before we begin. Please define to yourself clearly what your goal is by our doing this. What would you wish to accomplish by going on this journey?"

I allowed her a few moments of silent contemplation and when she said she was finished I brought her into hypnosis. I created a fairly deep trance and had her see herself on a familiar beach, somewhere the family had been to before. I had her experience being there with her different senses, seeing, hearing, and feeling all that surrounded her.

"This is a beautiful place...a nurturing place.... I'd like you to breathe in the tranquility...the beauty...the wholeness...the healing...of this place....

"You have been here before...but today it feels different.... There is a special energy in the air...a feeling of excitement...of expectancy.... It is like a gentle pulsation...or perhaps like a deep humming vibration.... It feels good.... It is energizing.... Can you feel that special feeling surrounding you...enveloping you?"

She nodded and I continued, "You know something special will happen today...or maybe tomorrow...or the day after...but something special will happen...in this place of healing....

"As you stand there...perhaps a gentle breeze is caressing you...or the sun is warming your back...and the special feeling increases...more and more...more and more.... You visualize a figure in the distance getting closer...and closer...as the special feeling gets stronger...and stronger.... You know who is coming to meet you.... You have waited a long time for this special moment.... He is coming so close...you can almost make out his features.... Let me know when you can make out his features...."

I waited for her to indicate that he was there and close enough for her to see who he was. Otherwise, I had no way of knowing if she visualized him or not. When she nodded again, I continued.

"You have been waiting for this to happen...for this opportunity...to say what you need to say...what you want to say.... When he comes close to you...and you can see the expression on his face...tell him how happy you are...to see him.... Listen carefully to his answer.... And then tell him...what you have wanted to say...for so long...."

I remained completely silent, allowing enough time for her experience to unfold. I knew something was happening by the varied expressions that crossed her features. When she began crying and using the tissues I had conveniently left for her, I knew that something powerful had taken place. At this point I still could not tell if it had been a positive or, *chas v'shalom*, a negative experience. I waited with bated breath until she visibly relaxed. A gentle smile graced her lips. The time seemed right for her to emerge from hypnosis. Very quietly, I began speaking again.

"And now…it is time to conclude your visit…with your special visitor…. If there is anything else…you wish to say…say it now…before you part…."

When she seemed ready, I brought her slowly out of hypnosis. She opened her eyes, wiped away her tears, and blew her nose before she looked at me. Her expression was one of wonder, disbelief, and utter exuberance.

"Welcome back!" I gave her a wide smile. "How was your trip?"

"Amazing! Extraordinary! Unreal! I don't know what else to call it, but there really are no words to describe it. I almost can't believe it myself."

"Have a drink of water and take some deep breaths." I handed her a glass of water and waited till she seemed more settled, more grounded.

"Would you like to share?" I asked. "You don't have to if you don't feel like it. I realize that your experience might be too personal to share with others."

"I can't tell you everything we said, but it was like magic happening. You are a genius to have done this for me!"

"I'll be very honest," I responded, "I often don't know what to do with clients, but Hashem gives me the intuition, the inspiration, and, of course, the ability. I am just a conduit for things to happen."

"Call it what you want, but I can't thank you enough for this happening, if that's the right word for it! Who would have ever thought that doing this was possible?"

"Doing what?" I asked very naively. "I hope you realize that I have no idea of what happened."

"Oh! Of course!" she laughed. "It felt as though you were there on the beach with me. But obviously you weren't watching a video of what was going on in my mind!"

She turned serious again as she contemplated what she had just been through. She seemed to be searching for the right words.

"It's an experience that I really can't describe," she finally said, "but it feels as though I put down this heavy yoke I was carrying on my shoulders. I was shlepping this burden for so long, it was compressing my insides. It made it hard for me to breathe, to digest my food, to activate my immune system, and suddenly, after a few minutes of talking to my father that heavy load was gone.

"All I said was how sorry I felt, how much I regretted having done and said certain things.... He looked beautiful, nothing like the way he looked when he died. He was so understanding, so warm, and his expression filled me with love.... And then he asked me to forgive him for the harsh interchanges between us. And in a split second, all the bad feelings were gone, disappeared, vanished into thin air.... He so much wanted me to heal and I asked him to intercede on high for me in whichever way he could.... There was nothing but love and pure connection between us. I could feel his love like a healing tonic inside my body.... I knew it was clearing out toxic stuff. I felt cleansed, renewed."

She sat silent and I rejoiced just looking at the glow she was exuding.

"You look awesome!" I commented. "I'm really glad for you, for this uplifting experience! By the way, how long do you think you were on the beach?"

"Um...maybe ten minutes."

"It was actually about twenty-five minutes," I said, as I showed her my watch.

"Are you serious!" she exclaimed. "It felt like so much less!"

"That's an indication of time distortion, and a sign of a good hypnotic trance. Do you have anything else to say or ask before we end today?"

"It felt so real. I'm convinced now that he forgave me a long time ago!" Bella said in a trembling voice.

"That's right. There is no resentment or vengeance in the world of truth. And your positive intentions and efforts by taking this journey can only bring good into your life."

I set up her next appointment and she left. We were going to meet in another four days, but surprisingly Bella called me the following night.

"Bracha, you won't believe this!" she said breathlessly.

"Believe what?" My curiosity was roused.

"It's unreal, but you know what happened?"

"No, please tell me!"

"This morning, Rafi called me! He said he wanted to ask my forgiveness and reconcile. He was so sorry for the split between us. He actually came to the house today, the first time in maybe six years!"

"I am flabbergasted!" was all I could say, and I was not exaggerating one bit. I was truly astounded.

"Tell he, how did his change of mind happen?" I wanted to know.

This was the amazing tale she told. "Rafi was having some difficulties in life and was deeply troubled. He needed advice from a Torah luminary and decided to visit one of the great *mekubalim* in the south. He was there last night, several hours after our session. He was told to write his name and his mother's name on a piece of paper and give it to the *mekubal* when he was called in. When Rafi gave the holy man the piece of paper, he looked at the names and said, 'Go home and make peace. After you do that you can come back.' That is all he would say.

"When Rafi came home, he knew what he had to do. This morning he called, and we got together. And we made peace, after all this time! Right after I made peace with my father! It seems impossible but it actually happened!"

"With Hashem, the impossible becomes possible and the extraordinary becomes ordinary!" I declared emphatically. "What do you think created this change in him?"

"I have no doubt that making peace with my father had something to do with it. There is no other explanation."

"It's the boomerang effect," I explained. "The *chessed* that we do brings down more *chessed* from above; forgiveness brings forgiveness and peace beings peace. That's the way Hashem set up the world. *Baruch Hashem*, you were able to reap the benefits of your endeavor in bringing about peace. May this open the gateway to even more peace and serenity in your life." I had seen this concept written in our holy texts in numerous places and felt that I could safely give her this explanation.

I had never studied Kabbalah, and, *l'havdil elef havdalos*, I had no knowledge of quantum physics. There was no way I could explain what actually happened, but the "boomerang effect" was a good general explanation. This episode clearly revealed to me that energy attracts like energy, as though magnets were pulling together.

Had I heard this story from someone else I might have been skeptical as to its veracity. But I heard it firsthand from the one it happened to. Over the time that I knew her, Bella continued telling me how her newfound relationship with Rafi was blossoming. And so I knew that this unbelievable story actually took place.

Bella lived a few more healthy and happy years before succumbing to her illness. They were years of flourishing as she basked in the delight of her renewed loving relationships. It seems that she had fulfilled her *tafkid* in this world and so her time to leave had come.

8

EMPOWERMENT

Kaila Leiner

Once a year I would go to Zurich, Switzerland, to run stress-management workshops. Almost invariably, I would get some private clients from the participants afterward. Kaila Leiner was one of them.

She had been married for twelve years and had five children. She suffered quite a bit from her mother-in-law, who, as she expressed it, "treats me like a nobody." She divulged that she didn't get the jewelry that her sisters-in-law received, her family was invited for Shabbos much less often than the others, and, even in public, was the target of her mother-in-law's disparaging remarks. In sum, she said, she felt despised.

"Since we have to go to my in-laws for *chagim* and sometimes for Shabbos," Kaila continued, "I try my best to treat her with respect. I bring her gifts, and I always cook or bake something whenever we come. I try so hard, but it never seems to make a difference. It's so difficult to speak to her without expressing the anger I feel inside!"

"That sounds like a really big challenge, Kaila," I offered empathetically. "Does your mother-in-law treat your husband in the same way?"

"If he tries to take my side and defend me, she'll say something nasty to him. Otherwise, she treats him more or less like the others. Most of the time, he doesn't say anything in my defense since he doesn't want to anger her."

"What about your father-in-law? How does he treat you?" I wanted to know.

"He's a sweet man and treats me nicely in private. I can see that he feels sorry for me. But he's totally dominated by his wife and never opposes her."

"Can you give me an example of some disparaging remark she said to you?"

"We were there for Shavuos, and two of my husband's siblings came as well. In front of everyone she said, 'Oh, Kaila, is this the new dress you bought? It makes you look so heavy. You look like you gained ten kilos since I saw you last. You'd better not eat the cheesecake tomorrow!'

"I could see my nieces snickering to themselves. Can you imagine what I felt like?" she lamented. "I wanted to run out of the room, but of course, I just stood there silently fuming. And I can give you dozens of other examples if you want!"

"No, this example is quite enough. I see clearly what you mean. This is a very painful situation. Since I can't change your mother-in-law, what exactly would you like to gain from our sessions?"

She sat silently for a minute, looking off into the distance. Then she turned to me and said, "I simply don't want to feel such pain and embarrassment when she says things like that. I'd also like to control my anger and learn to let it fade away like 'water off a duck's back.' I know it sounds like a lot, but that's what I want to achieve by coming to you. Am I being unrealistic?"

"Your goals are certainly legitimate. Whether we achieve 100 percent success or only 75 percent is impossible for me to say, but you certainly can make great strides in changing your feelings."

I was implying that we would achieve a fair amount of success, just that the exact amount was yet to be discovered. Implication is a tool used liberally in Ericksonian, or indirect, hypnosis.

"How?" she asked with a quizzical look on her face. "How can you get me to change my feelings? After all, she is saying those horrible things about me!"

I reflected deeply before answering. "I never have a set formula for what to do when I first begin working with a client. Hashem gives me *siyata d'Shmaya* and a fair amount of intuition. As we work together, I get a clearer picture of what is the best way to proceed. Naturally, you have no obligation to continue seeing me if you feel dissatisfied with the results we attain. But I believe some change for the better is preferable to none."

"Of course, of course! So let's get started."

"I want to know more about your mother-in-law, to try to figure out what makes her say things like that. Do you know anything about her childhood, her parents and siblings? Tell me whatever you know."

"Her parents were Holocaust survivors. They married in Switzerland and had two daughters, Gitta and Rina, and an only son. Gitta, my mother-in-law, is the oldest, her brother Yankel is next, and Rina is the youngest. Rina is a nice woman, beautiful, intelligent and is married to the rabbi of a local shul. He is real a *talmid chacham*. I think my mother-in-law is insanely jealous of her because she can say unkind things about her, not to her face, but behind her back."

"Do you know how your husband's grandparents treated their daughters and their only son? Do you know of any traumatic or disturbing incidents?" I felt intuitively that Gitta Leiner's behavior was linked to her childhood.

Kaila searched her memory but could not come up with anything that seemed significant. I suggested that she ask her husband if he remembered conversations or happenings from visits to his grand-parents or from things he'd heard his parents saying that might throw light on the situation.

"Yes," she said, "Rudy, my husband, might have some memories from his grandparent's home. He loved them a lot and went often to visit before they passed away.... Oh, I remember now. Rudy would joke sometimes about his aunt Rina, calling her 'Grand Daddy's girl.'"

I continued threshing out the subject until it seemed apparent that Mrs. Leiner had an inferiority complex, most likely because she felt less loved than the others, namely the only son and the sweet baby of the family. My hunch was that this caused her to become assertive and aggressive in her attempt to cover up her feelings of inadequacy. She felt compelled to have complete rule of the roost. Instead of acting out on all the members of her family, somehow Kaila had become the scapegoat, the sacrificial lamb, receiving the brunt of her mother-in-law's attacks. I knew now what I had to do to help my client get the control she needed to modify her feelings.

"Kaila, when someone acts in an obnoxious manner," I explained, "we have to ask ourselves, why? There is always a reason why people do what they do. Their reason might not be a very good one, but it acts as a justification for them to do certain things that normally they would not do. It prevents them from seeing the hurt they are inflicting on others in their attempt to help themselves.

"You have become the *korban* of your mother-in-law and, you know what, probably your mother-in-law was the *korban* in her family. It seems to me that in her mixed-up way, she is trying to regain what she feels she lost as a child growing up in her parent's home. I don't know how much she suffered, but it might have been an awful lot. It is a clearly documented fact that children of Holocaust survivors often suffer from psychological problems. So we can assume that she did suffer, and her present hurtful behavior is most likely an outcome of that. Probably, if we questioned your father-in-law and your husband's siblings, we would discover numerous indications to prove our hypothesis. Kaila, just as I can empathize with you in your suffering, I can also empathize with her in her suffering."

I watched Kaila carefully for her reaction to my words. I expected to see some resistance in her accepting what I was implying, that she, too, should empathize with her mother-in-law's suffering. Her reaction wasn't long in coming.

"What! Are you saying that because she suffered as a child, she has the right to make me the scapegoat of the family?"

"Certainly not. I'm not talking about right and wrong at this moment. I'm merely trying to point out the most likely reasons for why she is acting this way. Instead of seeing her as an evil person trying her best to hurt you, we can see her acting out because of her own unmet needs and unresolved pain. Then her actions become understandable, and subsequently we feel less angry.

"This is the basis of the mitzvah of being *dan l'chaf zechus*, of judging people favorably. The commandment to give people the benefit of the doubt is not merely a nice thing to do. It is an obligation. Hashem wants us to find believable reasons for why others do things that are or appear to be wrong, so that we can be more forgiving, understanding, and even empathetic. And we fulfill the mitzvah even if we come up with the wrong reason for someone's 'bad' behavior, because we now feel less antagonistic toward that person. Does this make sense to you?"

She sat quietly for a few moments looking down. She then raised her head and seemed to inflate like an angry rooster, as she let loose her reply with emotion.

"OK, I see your point. But that doesn't mean she is right in doing what she does to me or that she shouldn't be punished for it! If I had the choice, I would never step into her house again!"

"I totally understand," I answered evenly. "It's a tough situation to be in. But since you will find yourself in her home from time to time, let's work on a way for you to feel less hurt and angry and, hopefully, even somewhat forgiving. Would you like to do that?"

"Sure, 'less hurt and angry.' But leave out the 'forgiving' part."

"Fine.... Make yourself comfortable in the chair...."

I spent a long time on the hypnotic induction to give her a chance to let go of her pent-up anger. When she appeared quite relaxed, I did several tests, gaging her level of hypnosis. I wished to induce a fairly deep trance state. When I felt she was ready, I began the therapy.

"See yourself now walking outside.... You find yourself in a small playground.... There is only one little girl there.... The others have gone home for lunch.... You come close and notice that she is crying.... She is young...maybe five or six years old.... She is sobbing and covering her face with her hands.... You sit down on the bench near where she is standing.... You feel so sorry for this little child.... She's all alone.... Maybe she is lost....

"Ask her why she is crying...."

I was silent, giving her a chance to imagine asking the child what is wrong.

"Did she tell you why she is crying?"

Kaila shook her head in the negative.

"Maybe she is ashamed.... Ask her what her name is."

"She said, Gitty."

"Do you think you could make her feel better?.... Can you comfort her in some way?"

She nodded and I waited for her to imagine soothing the child.

"How does she respond to you?" I wanted to know if the child resisted or allowed Kaila to calm her down.

"I put my arms around her...and stroked her.... At first she stood there stiffly...but soon she put her arms around me...." She spoke slowly, a sign of deep trance.

"Is she still crying?"

"No...she stopped."

"Can you put her on the bench next to you?"

Kaila nodded.

"Tell her you want...to be her friend...and help her."

I waited a few moments. "How does she respond?"

"She's smiling...and laughing.... She says she wants to be my friend."

"Ask her again...why she was crying."

I waited for a bit and then asked, "Please tell me what she told you...."

"I don't know...how to go home."

"Ask her how she got to the playground...."

After a moment, she replied, "My mother brought me here...and left me."

"Ask her why her mother left her."

"Because I was naughty...."

"Ask her why she was naughty."

"Because I took the toys away...from the baby."

"Ask her if she likes the baby."

"She said, 'No, I hate the baby!.... Mommy kisses her...and plays with her all day...and makes me put away the toys.... Today when I was naughty...Mommy said she doesn't want me anymore.... She left me here all alone.'.... She's crying again."

"Comfort her like you did before.... Tell her you'll bring her home...and speak to her mother...."

I continued encouraging Kaila to befriend the child and, most importantly, to elicit her compassion for the unfortunate little girl. Once I brought her out of trance, I suggested that Kaila visit Gitty in her imagination several times a week in a quiet state of relaxation and to help her in whichever way she could. She agreed to come to the playground to meet with Gitty three times a week, and play or go on walks with her, as well as becoming a listening ear for Gitty's woes.

I explained to Kaila that by befriending the child she would be doing herself a favor as well.

"Hashem has set up universal laws in the world and we are told that when one bestows compassion, and when one does kindness, he receives the same in return. Kaila, you can be curious in discovering in which ways your life will change for the better after your efforts at eliciting kindness and compassion."

Kaila was not convinced. "But I'm only helping her in my mind and not doing anything in the real world.... How can that make a difference?"

"You are where your mind is!" I answered with conviction. "By imagining yourself a person of *chessed*, you become one! By imagining yourself giving the benefit of the doubt, it will affect you in actuality. And your life will change accordingly. Try it and discover for yourself if this is true or not."

"OK. I said already that I would imagine meeting with Gitty three times a week. I just didn't really believe that it would do anything for me."

I made clear to Kaila that it did not matter if our imaginary scenario was true or not, or if Gitty's mother was abusive or not. What mattered were the feelings in Kaila's heart and mind toward the child. Automatically, without her even realizing it, that would change her feelings for the adult Gitta. We ended the session with a commitment from Kaila to meet with the unfortunate little Gitty. Time would tell if it made a difference or not.

At the following session, Kaila was all smiles and enthusiasm. She recounted several phone conversations she had had with her mother-in-law that had been decidedly more positive than what she was accustomed to.

"But our improved relationship was just on the phone," she added. "I'm not sure what will happen when I see her or when she sees me. Maybe the old feelings will come up again. I still wish I wouldn't have to go there for Shabbos!"

"I quite understand." I wanted Kaila to feel how clearly I understood her doubts and hesitations. "'Rome wasn't built in a day,' they say, and life doesn't change over the period of one week."

She nodded her head in agreement with my assessment of the situation.

"I'm going to teach you a simple technique that will enable you to feel safe and protected when you are in your mother-in-law's house, or, as a matter of fact, when you are in any unpleasant environment. Would you like that?"

"Absolutely! If you could do that, it would be amazing!"

"We feel discomfort, threatened, or put down as a result of our perceptions. If we change our perceptions, we change the way we feel."

Kaila's puzzled expression prompted me to say, "You don't have to understand everything I am saying now, for in a moment you will feel that what I am saying is totally true. Just allow yourself to let go and travel with me on a short journey that we will take together."

I put Kaila into a light trance. She was a willing subject and I saw her tension melting away as she followed my cues leading her into a state of relaxation.

"We know that Hashem loves us and protects us.... Sometimes we need to suffer...for our ultimate benefit.... We trust that Hashem knows what He is doing with us...and why He puts us through our difficulties....

"If we can feel that Hashem is there with us...in our *tzarah*...'*imo anochi b'tzarah*'[iv].... Hashem says, 'I am with you in your suffering.'....If we feel that we are not alone...then we go through the challenge...completely differently.... We don't have to protect ourselves because we know that Hashem is protecting us.... He will never abandon us...and whatever is happening to us is exactly what needs to happen...for our ultimate growth and fulfillment...."

I continued with my hypnotic patter for another short while, nudging Kaila gently into a deeper relaxed state, until I felt that she was ready to move on to the next piece of the journey.

"Because you are sure that Hashem is always there with you...and that He wants you to succeed in overcoming your challenges...in the best way possible...He responds to your request for help...when you ask for it....

"When you are in an uncomfortable environment...and ask for protection from feeling hurt or shamed...all you have to do is say, 'Hashem, please send me Your shield of protection'.... Then you will notice something like a tent coming down from *Shamayim*...and completely enveloping you....It is a shield of Divine light...straight from Hashem...that has the ability to protect you...like a shield of armor.... This shield of light is strong...stronger than diamonds...and nothing can penetrate it.... Nothing can penetrate this shield...if you don't want it to.... No one can enter inside of it...unless you let them in.... You are fully and totally protected by this Divine shield of protection...this shield of light...because it comes from Hashem and is stronger...than anything in this world...."

I let the message sink in for a few moments.

"When you want this protection...all you do is look to Heaven...and ask Hashem to send it to you...and you will see and feel it...surrounding you.... Once you are inside the shield...you are with Hashem...taking care of you.... You can feel how good it feels to be there...protected and loved...and taken care of...and safe....

"I want you now to feel that feeling.... And to know...that you can be safe and protected whenever you wish.... I want you now...to ask Hashem to send you His shield of protection.... Look up to *Shamayim* and ask Hashem to send down...His shield of protection.... Tell me when you feel surrounded by it.... Let me know with a nod of your head when it is there...."

I waited until she nodded.

"Good! Hashem is here with you...inside the shield.... Now feel the warmth...the love...the caring...the guidance...the protection...the safety...inside this shield.... Hashem wants to protect you...wants to enable you...to overcome your challenges.... You are not doing this alone.... You are doing this together with Hashem.... Let me know just how good you feel...."

She spoke slowly, expressing the way she felt.

"I want you to repeat to yourself...three times, 'I am safe and protected...inside Hashem's shield of protection.... In here...no one can hurt me.'"

She repeated the words three times.

"Good! Excellent! Now you will learn to bring the shield down...instantly by using an anchor...by pressing your thumb and forefinger of your right hand together each time you say the words...'Hashem, please send me Your shield of protection'...."

I taught her the anchor technique, and had her repeat it several times until I knew she could do it on her own easily and effortlessly.

"Great! Excellent! You are doing absolutely wonderful!.... Do you feel completely safe and protected inside the shield?"

I wanted to hear Kaila say it again, to be sure she had no doubts about it.

"Yes...completely safe and protected...inside the shield," she said.

"You can bring into your shield of protection anything you like...maybe pictures on the walls...or a plant...or music...whatever you like...to make you feel at home and happy...."

She smiled as she imagined doing what I had suggested.

"Only you know that the shield is there...no one else can see it...but you see and feel it....Maybe it has a shine or a glow...at the edges of the shield...like an egg surrounding you...and the edges have a luminescence that you can see...but no one else can see.... Can you give your shield a shine or glow to its edges?"

She nodded again.

"Now we are going to see...just how well the shield of protection is able to protect you.... When people say nasty things to us...the words are like arrows...trying to pierce our flesh...our heart...and hurt us...."

"When an arrow hits a shield...that is stronger than it is...the arrow breaks from the impact...and falls harmlessly to the ground.... Is that not true?"

She nodded in agreement.

"Now, I want you to see yourself in some place that feels unpleasant.... You use your anchor now...to bring down your shield of protection.... Is it in place surrounding you completely?"

I waited for her nod.

"You feel safe and protected.... Feel that feeling now...."

I waited and she murmured that she feels safe.

"You see someone approaching from the distance.... You see her taking out a bow and arrow...and aiming in your direction.... Since you are safe and protected...and inside the shield with Hashem...Who is taking care of you...you have no fear...no discomfort.... You know that the arrow cannot penetrate the shield...because the shield is stronger than diamonds.... It is a shield than only you can see...no one else sees it...but you know that it is there.... You can see and feel it around you...with its glow at the edges.... And you feel the safe and protective atmosphere...that you are surrounded with....

"Now watch...as the arrow is shot at you...and hits the shield...and breaks upon impact...and falls harmlessly to the ground...."

I gave her time to imagine the scene and then continued speaking.

"You feel so happy that you are safe and protected...and nothing can penetrate the shield.... You might feel sorry...for someone who wishes to shoot arrows at you.... Why does she feel she needs to do that?.... She cannot harm you...because you are inside the shield...with Hashem...safe and protected....But you feel sorry for her...that she is acting this way.... Maybe she had a hard life...and was shot at by someone else...and she thinks this is the way to be...the only way to be.... You won't judge her...but just feel distant...and safe and protected...."

I had her imagine several different scenarios and had her experience the safety, the inability to be hurt, by using the anchor and bringing her shield of protection to surround her. I reinforced her belief that nothing could penetrate the shield, unless Hashem decided so, and if Hashem wanted to help her through her challenge, He would allow the shield to protect her completely. After an appropriate amount of time, I brought her out of hypnosis.

"How do you feel?" I asked as she opened her eyes and stretched.

"It seemed so real!" Kaila exclaimed. "I am amazed at the power of that shield. I had absolutely no fear, no doubts that I would be protected. It was like magic!"

"It is simply a matter of perception," I added. "If you believe you will be protected, you will be. Now, if an actual lion was running toward you, I would not use this shield to protect you! I would use my legs to run just as fast as I possibly could! But when it comes to words, to attitudes, to beliefs, use the shield and you will come out the better person for it!"

"Amazing, amazing!" she repeated in somewhat of a daze.

"I want you to continue with visiting Gitty at least three times a week, taking care of her in the best way you can. You will discover that the arrows you have been subjected to until now will not be shot at you in the same way as before. You can even be curious to discover if they will, over time, disappear completely."

Kaila wanted another session, just to be sure, although I felt that she had already completed the work. But since repetition is so important when it comes to hypnosis, I knew another session for reinforcement would only benefit her.

After a few weeks, she called me to say that her life was decidedly improved. Her mother-in-law still shot arrows at her from time to time, but Kaila felt so unaffected by them that she was able to visit her in-laws' home without apprehension. She found that what her mother-in-law was unable to give her—love, respect, and appreciation—her husband started giving her in abundance. Kaila had become such a positive personality despite the negative circumstances she had to endure that he could not help but express those feelings to her, the feelings she so desperately craved. Not only did the relationship between mother-in-law and daughter-in-law improve, but the *shalom bayis* between Kaila and her husband reached new heights.

Suzy Halpern

On my return from Boston to Monsey after attending a hypnosis conference, I called my friend Miriam to tell her about the amazing time I had experienced. After hearing all about the hypnosis "miracles" I had witnessed, Miriam told me that her niece was suffering with depression and asked if I could help her. I answered that I was not a medical practitioner, and if the girl required medical attention, she needed to be treated by the appropriate professionals. Miriam said she would talk to her sister and find out more details about the situation.

It took but a few days before my friend's sister Janet called me up. It was about Suzy, her twenty-two-year-old daughter. Suzy was actually Janet's niece, whom she had adopted after Suzy's parents,

Janet's brother and sister-in-law, were killed in a car accident. They had adopted Suzy's younger brother at the same time. Both children had been quite small then and for all practical purposes Janet was Suzy's mother and Suzy was Janet's daughter.

Suzy was being treated by a psychiatrist, who had put her on several medications for depression, and she was also doing talk therapy. Janet reported that at this time, Suzy was much more stable than she had been in the last several years and was even able to hold down a job. However, she was missing a zest for life and found it hard to deal with the simple routine of daily life. She wondered if I could teach her some coping skills.

My first question to Janet was, "Is Suzy at all suicidal?"

"Not now. She has been in the past, but as I said, she is quite stable now. She's been at her current job for the last year and a half."

"That sounds good. I'm happy to take Suzy on if you get your psychiatrist's permission for her to work with me. I don't need his approval of my methods; I simply need to hear that he feels it is safe for her to do hypnosis with someone certified in hypnotherapy. Tell him I do not intend to dig into her past to look for the reasons behind her depression. I merely wish to teach her positive thinking and stress-management skills."

Once I had the doctor's consent to work with Suzy, I took on the challenge with mounting curiosity. *In which way will I be able to help this young lady?* I wondered.

Suzy walked in to my office slowly for our first session. She appeared disheveled, her hair in disarray and her clothes decidedly out of fashion. I assumed her mother was not telling her to brush her hair or laying out clothes for her as she would for a young child. She probably wanted Suzy to take responsibility for her appearance and for herself in general, and I agreed with that approach. But before Suzy could or would take responsibility for being her best self she would need to learn to appreciate and cherish that self. Perhaps she needed to learn to love that self as well.

"Hi, Suzy," I said cheerily. "Make yourself comfortable. Would you like a drink?'

"No thanks," she responded in a voice devoid of emotion. "I have my water bottle."

"So how would you like me to help you?" I wanted to know.

"I'm on this medication and it makes me sleepy. It's hard for me to get up in the morning and then I come late to work."

"Did you mention this to your doctor? Perhaps the dose can be reduced."

"My mom spoke to him and we're reducing the amount slowly. He said he might take me off one drug soon if he continues to see me improving. That might help the sleepiness."

"That sounds encouraging," I said. "Tell me about yourself. What other things bother you or create situations that are hard for you to deal with?"

"I sometimes get panic attacks. It's hard for me to breathe and it feels like I'm passing out."

"Do you know what brings them on?" I was beginning to realize that I had a complicated case to deal with in this young lady.

"No. I really have no idea. They come whenever they feel like it."

I suspected that there was something that triggered them, but I would have to discover what that was at a later time. For now, I'd have to give her some "first aid" techniques for dealing with them.

"What do you do when you have an attack?" I needed to know what strategies she was using and if they were helpful or not.

"I don't do anything. My therapist taught me that I just have to wait it out and I need to know that they will pass and that nothing will happen to me."

"How often do they come?"

"Um...not that often. Maybe once in a few weeks."

"Good to hear that! Now, would you like to learn to do something that will make you feel better while you wait it out?"

"Sure."

"Normally, in different situations in life, there is a fleeting moment that alerts you that something is about to happen, but it hasn't started yet. Let's take leg cramps, for example. Have you ever had one of those?"

She nodded in the affirmative.

"Usually you can feel the muscle tightening before it hurts and you know that the cramp is coming, right?"

She nodded again.

"Sometimes if you start stretching out the muscle and massaging it right away, you can stop the cramp from getting worse and it goes away."

"Yeah, right."

"I'm going to teach you to do something that will stop the panic attack from coming on full force and it will go away real fast."

"Really?"

"Yes, and it's much easier than you think. The first thing you have to do is pay attention to when it begins. There is a very small moment when you know that it's coming but you still don't feel any discomfort."

"I never noticed that."

"I know," I answered. "And that's because you weren't looking for that moment. But I assure you that it is there. As soon as you learn to recognize that moment, you begin the special exercises that I'm going to teach you."

"Cool, let's do it!"

I was glad to hear some enthusiasm in her voice. It sounded as though she were waking up from a state of stupor.

I first taught her the *"re-laaaax"* breathing technique. I had her practice it long enough until I could see her visibly relaxing as she did it. I then taught her "box breathing," a more complicated type of breathing that would be more useful for her in high states of anxiety.

Once she could comfortably perform both breathing exercises, I taught her the anchor technique. She had a hard time coming up with a joyful, empowering memory, but once she did, she really enjoyed bringing on the happy feelings as she pressed her fingers together. We spent quite a bit of time doing it, as I wanted this technique to become second nature and her immediate go-to whenever she felt overwhelmed.

"Suzy, you have learned some very powerful strategies today for helping yourself. You can use them not only when you have a panic attack, but in many different situations. Anytime you feel greatly stressed, anxious, or angry use the box breathing. You will calm down almost immediately. And when you feel only a little stressed and wish to become more deeply relaxed, use the *"re-laaaax"* breathing. You can use it also for helping yourself to fall asleep. And whenever you want to change your feelings of sadness or depression or fear or any negative state of mind to a happy state of mind, you will use your anchor. But, in order for the anchor to be very effective and work instantly, you must practice it many times every day."

"How often should I do it?"

"At least five times a day. You will need to be in a quiet, private place, so that you can bring up your happy memory without any disturbances. Do you have your own room?"

"Yes."

"Excellent. So you should go to your room, telling your mother and siblings not to bother you, and practice there. You can actually practice anywhere at all, as long as you are not disturbed. Once you get so used to doing this and are able to bring up the happy state of mind easily and effortlessly, you will find that you will be able to take control of your panic attacks. You might even be able to stop them in their tracks just by doing the breathing exercise."

"Are you serious?" She looked incredulous.

"Do I look like someone that would mislead you? Your success will depend on how much you practice. The breathing exercises should be practiced at least for five minutes, three times a day. You can do them anywhere, on the bus or at work and before falling asleep. The more you practice, the quicker you will see results. You are breaking old patterns in your brain and replacing them with new patterns, by creating new neural pathways. Think about a habit. No one is born with a habit; they are created by repetition. And this is what you will be doing during the next week, creating new habits."

I let the idea sink in. Then I asked, "On a scale from zero to one hundred, how committed, in percentages, are you to doing this?"

"Um...maybe 50 to 60 percent."

I knew that wasn't good enough. She would not have the energy to practice, nor would she do so consistently with that kind of commitment. I needed her to want to do this so badly, that she would say she was committed 95 percent or more. My job now was to magnify her motivation.

"Close your eyes and make yourself comfortable in the chair...."

I took my time putting her into a light trance, even though our session was almost over.

The rewards of going overtime were well worth it, as I wanted her to enjoy the experience of being in trance, of feeling relaxed, at peace, and being taken care of. I wanted her to savor this experience; I wanted her to want to come back for more. And, of course, I wanted to amplify her motivation to carry out any suggestions I would be offering her.

"You are a precious, beloved child of Hashem....You are so unique, so special to Him...and He wants to give you what you need.... He wants to give you, His child...whatever will help you succeed.... You have a unique mission in life...and He wants to help you achieve that unique mission.... You now know that you have the ability to fulfill your mission because Hashem wants you to succeed and He will help you do that...."

I allowed a lengthy pause before continuing.

"Now imagine yourself as a small child...a small princess...sitting on your father's lap...the king's lap...playing with him.... He is happy to play with you...because he loves you so much.... Now, ask him for what you need...what you want."

I asked her to see him giving her gifts that a child might ask for, such as a doll or a hair ribbon. Then I had her imagine herself resting her head on his chest, feeling his arms embracing her securely. The goal was for her to feel safe and secure, loved and cherished. Imagining herself as the king's daughter, she could receive whatever it was she needed, as her father the king was not limited in any way. This could only boost her self-esteem and her belief that she could accomplish whatever she needed to. I then asked her to imagine her reserves of motivation growing and growing inside of her.

"You can now see inside your brain...the part of your brain where motivation resides.... You notice a tank with the word 'Motivation' written on it. You look inside and notice the liquid that is there....Notice the color of that 'motivation liquid'.... The color of the liquid gives you the feeling of motivation.... You notice that the tank is only half full.... You ask the King to fill the tank all the way to the top.... He does that for you.... Now that the tank is all full...*you* feel full of motivation...full of energy to do...whatever you need to do...."

I was silent, letting the feelings embed themselves in her brain. The message I imparted could be only as strong as the feelings that accompanied it were. Once Suzy had a strong feeling of motivation, I knew she would be more fully committed to doing her exercises.

I continued for a few more minutes enhancing her feelings of self-esteem and belief in her abilities. I reinforced her desire to do her exercises regularly and to make that an important goal in her life. I wanted to conclude the session by giving her a sense of accomplishment with everything that she was doing as a result of our time together. I had her imagine gold medals being pinned to her chest, attesting to her success. To end, I asked her to imagine standing in front of a mirror, tall, upright, smiling, enjoying the display of medals she had earned. I then slowly brought her out of hypnosis.

She opened her eyes but did not look at me. Her far-off gaze was focused on the opposite wall and she seemed to still be in trance.

"Welcome back, Suzy," I said, getting her to focus on me. "How do you feel?"

"It's a nice feeling," was her quiet reply. "Relaxed."

"Good. This is all very healing to your nervous system. And although your medication tends to make you sleepy, this type of relaxation will actually give you more energy. It will enable you to focus your reserves of energy on whatever you want to do each day. You'll feel more accomplished, with a greater sense of satisfaction."

"Sounds good."

"Tell me, Suzy, when I ask you once again, on a scale from zero to a hundred, how committed do you now feel to doing your exercises?"

She rolled her eyes up as she contemplated her answer. "I'd say it's probably a 90 or 95 percent now."

"Great! Wonderful. I'm really proud of you. I'm sure that within a few days you'll feel the benefit of what you are doing.

"What I'm going to ask you to do next might sound childish, but it's going to be really beneficial to you. I want you to buy yourself a new notebook. You can decorate the front cover if you want. This is going to be your "daily journal" notebook, and each day you'll write down which exercises you did, how often and for how much time. Let me make a sample page for you."

I took out a piece of paper and made a chart with the days of the week across the top of the page and the various exercises along the length. I told her to give herself a check for each exercise every time she practiced it that day. Potentially, she could earn sixty or more checks in one week if she practiced all her exercises three times daily every day.

"I'll be adding more tasks to your chart week by week. When you accumulate ten, twenty, thirty, or more checks, however many you decide, you'll buy yourself a gift, something you wouldn't normally get for yourself. How does this sound to you?"

"Sounds like fun, a bit of a challenge, but fun."

"Good. I want you to know that you can do whatever you put your mind to. And if you can see visually exactly what you did and what you did not do, you'll have the framework for guiding yourself to do more and more. I want you to go at your own pace, without pressure, and do what feels good and right for you each day. But as I said before, the more you practice, the faster you will feel better and in control of your moods and energy levels."

When Suzy returned the following week, she looked more alert than she had the previous time. When I asked her how her week had gone, she immediately pulled out her notebook and opened up to the first entry.

"Look," she said happily, "how much I practiced. I only skipped one day!"

The chart for the week had more than thirty checks. For each day of the week she had used a different color marker. I could sense her enthusiasm for performing the tasks I had given her.

"Great! Wonderful! I'm so proud of you! You're an amazing student!" I was responding to her as I would to a young child. It seemed that was what she needed, and she drank in my praise as parched soil would suck up life-giving water.

"Let me give you a hug!"

She allowed me to hug her and I felt her hug in return. I was grateful that I had gotten through to her and was tapping in to her needs.

"I knew that you were completely capable of doing this!"

I wanted to emphasize my belief in her abilities, although, truthfully, I never knew ahead of time how any client would respond to therapy. It depended on so many different factors. It had happened more than once when working with a client that we would move ahead beautifully week by week, and then "crash!"—we'd undergo a setback. And so, I never took progress for granted. And, therefore, I was truly encouraged by Suzy's positive response.

"Tell me," I said, "how many checks do you need in order to buy yourself a prize?"

"Twenty-two. I got more than that and bought myself something," was her proud reply.

"Super! What did you buy?"

"A set of pastels. I love to draw and somehow never seem to have the supplies on hand. I made a picture for my room."

"That's really beautiful! But tell me," I asked, "why did you pick twenty-two checks instead of just twenty?"

"At first I thought of choosing twenty, but then I said to myself, 'Let me make it a little bit harder than that.' I want to be able to exert myself a little more before I give myself a reward. So I chose a number for every year of my life."

"I'm truly amazed!" I was not exaggerating. I could not have asked for a better outcome to our therapy.

We spent the following weeks adding tasks to her chart. I reiterated that she was to go at her own pace, without having the pressure of feeling that "I must" or "I'm not good enough if I don't do it." I wanted her to do more because she actually wanted to and because the sense of accomplishment gave her a "buzz." The prizes she earned for herself added to the self-esteem I was building up, step by tiny step.

I wanted her to feel responsibility toward her job, and so, one task was going to bed earlier, enabling her to get up on time for work. Another aspect of our work was enhancing her self-respect. This was reflected in the tasks of keeping her room neat and clean, as well as her personal appearance. She did wonderfully in all these areas, but one. She admitted to me that she hated brushing her teeth and that she actually had not done so in perhaps the last few years.

Although I was shocked and perturbed by this behavior, I made light of it. It was an interesting phenomenon, this teeth brushing aversion. Over the years I had treated several clients who had an aversion to teeth brushing, nail cutting, and even shampooing their hair. I had my theory about what was behind it and had a fair amount of success in dealing with it. At this point in time with Suzy, I was not yet going to address the issue at all.

An area that proved to be a challenge for her was helping out at home. Her mother got back late after a tiring day of work and could have used some help with household chores. I wanted her to feel gratitude to her adoptive mother, as she was paying for her therapy out of sincere love and compassion for her suffering child. An important goal, in my opinion, was getting Suzy to be more "other-focused" rather than only working on self-improvement. The more she could focus in a positive way on others, the less she would feel her personal pain.

I was proud to see Suzy moving ahead in every area I gave her to work on. It was not always smooth sailing, and we had our ups and downs, sometimes taking two steps forward and then one back. But in general, we were moving forward. Every session ended with a hypnotic trance that reinforced whatever we had been talking about earlier. It helped her make the changes she was undergoing more automatic, accomplished easily and effortlessly, rather than her needing to use self-control and willpower to achieve them.

The satisfaction she felt by checking off her tasks on a daily basis helped enormously with improving her emotional state, in giving her more energy, and enabling her to have a deeper and more restful sleep. Her self-esteem was growing by leaps and bounds. I decided we had reached a point where I could safely challenge her with the teeth-brushing issue.

Toward the end of one session, I casually said, "Oh, by the way, Suzy, I don't mean to alarm you but I just read an article which is quite relevant to you. It was about dental hygiene. The author wrote that keeping the mouth clean and free of bacteria is enormously important as bacteria from the mouth can travel through the throat and then lodge in the heart muscle. This could affect the health of the heart.

"I'm sure you have a healthy heart because you never complained about it bothering you. But I think the time has come for you to do the proper *hishtadlus* to keep that heart healthy. The time has come for you to begin brushing your teeth. I know you can do it because you have been able to do all the other things you put your mind to. All you have to do is decide you want to do it.

'But I hate the feeling. It makes me anxious!"

"Would you be surprised if I told you that you could change the way you feel about it?"

"No. I don't think I would be surprised by anything you told me. The most unlikely things have been happening since we started our sessions. But I really don't want to brush my teeth!"

"Suzy, I'm not going to make you do anything, and you won't do anything that you don't want to do. If you do it, it will be because you decided you want to. It's completely up to you to decide. OK? Understood?"

"Yeah, I understand. I know you won't make me do anything. So what can you do to help me change my feelings?"

"Let's do a little relaxation session and see what we can come up with."

I put Suzy into a medium trance. I had her imagine that there were two Suzys. She experienced being a tiny version of herself standing inside the other Suzy's mouth.

"As you stand there...inside your mouth...you observe whatever is there.... You notice the walls of the room...their color.... Is it a pleasant color?.... Is it a healthy color?.... Are they smooth...or puffy...or are there sores...or abrasions...on the walls...or do they appear to be in fine condition?.... Tell me now what you observe?"

She spoke slowly with effort. "They are red...and blotchy...with bumps...."

"Look at the teeth.... Notice their color...and texture.... Are they smooth...or is there anything attached to them?.... Are there any holes...or do they appear to be in fine condition?.... Tell me now what you observe?"

"They have a yellowish color...also brown spots.... I see little holes.... Some pieces of food are stuck in them...."

I was pleased with her replies, probably close to reality, as she could have simply imagined that all looked fine. Her subconscious mind was being more honest than her conscious mind was. I continued with my questions.

"Now, pay attention to the smell in this room.... Is it a fresh and inviting smell...or is it an unpleasant one? Pay attention to whatever is here for you to see and observe...."

"Bad smell...ugly smell...."

"You notice that you are holding a brush in one hand.... It is just the right size for these teeth.... In the other hand is a tube of toothpaste.... Ask your teeth if they wish you...to give them a good brushing.... They will talk to you and tell you what they want...."

She took a while before she answered. "They don't want to be brushed.... But they told me to do it anyway...." She was expressing her internal resistance to begin brushing her teeth and, simultaneously, her success at overcoming it.

"Very good.... Now you will put the paste on the brush...and very, very gently...begin brushing...up and down...and in and out...and all around...all the teeth.... You can sing or hum to them...if you wish to make them feel good...as you brush...ever so gently...so lightly...so smoothly...making them feel so good...."

I allowed enough of a pause for her to imagine giving her teeth a thorough brushing.

"Your teeth look different now.... Tell me how they look."

"White...shiny...fresh.... They smell fresh...."

"Excellent. You did a very good job.... I know those teeth are happy...with the brushing you gave them.... Listen to them now...telling you how good they feel...how happy they are...and how much they thank you...for the nice job you did...to make them look and feel so great.... Listen to them telling you how they feel."

I could see her facial expression change as she "heard" her teeth talking to her. It appeared to me that they were giving her a high five.

"Do your teeth...want another brushing?" I wanted to know.

"I'll ask.... They said yes."

"Will you be able to make them happy again...and give them another brushing?"

"Maybe."

After a short while I brought her out of trance. She stretched and looked around the room.

"How do you feel, Suzy?" I asked.

"That was the weirdest thing! Talking teeth!"

"It's just a way for you to imagine what your teeth might be feeling if they had feelings. If they had feelings, they surely would have been grateful to you for making them clean and healthy."

"But it still seems so weird."

"You know, since your teeth can't actually talk to you, doing this is a good way for you to get to know what they would want if they could talk. Now, I'm not telling you to begin brushing your teeth. I want you to go at your own pace. When you will feel ready, you'll do it. There's no pressure or deadline, just whenever you feel you can that's when you'll do it. You might be curious to discover just how soon you will feel ready to do it." I was implying, with my last sentence, that she would want to do it.

I told her to add the teeth-brushing task to her journal and whenever she was ready, she'd be able to give herself a check.

I was more than a little surprised when she came the following week with the good news that she had started brushing her teeth. I didn't expect it would happen that soon, and I felt as excited as she did with her success.

"And it's not as bad as I thought it would be," she told me happily. "I actually like looking at them in the mirror and seeing them clean and shiny."

I didn't ask her if her teeth were thanking her, as she would have thought that was "weird," but I had a suspicion that they were.

The next step was to get her to take more responsibility for her future.

Suzy was working at a menial job that she didn't particularly enjoy. I wanted to know what type of work would give her joy.

"I'd like to work with babies and maybe with learning-disabled children. I have a learning-disabled nephew and I have a good way with him. I also love to paint and draw, and I make all kinds of crafts."

"What type of training do you need in order to work with babies or learning-disabled children? Which type of work would give you the opportunity to use your talents of painting, drawing, and craft making?"

We threshed out various options. She finally decided that what she most wanted to become was an art therapist working with learning-disabled children, but not with emotionally challenged ones. I told her to do some homework and find out which courses were available close to home that would give her the certification she needed. We were working on long-range plans now, which was challenging work indeed.

After a couple of weeks, she came back with the information we needed. She realized she would have to work at some kind of job in order to finance her plans until she was ready and able to work in the field she was training for. She decided she could do alterations as she enjoyed using the sewing machine and that would bring in income relatively easily. And she could take some simple sewing jobs from her neighbor who owned a dress boutique and created the dresses she sold. She would also do babysitting whenever she could. And hopefully, she could sell her crafts and jewelry at local fairs.

All these proposed plans were wonderful, but we realized that the income she could generate would not be enough to pay for her education. She then asked her uncle if he would give her an interest-free loan for the next ten years. Once he agreed and worked out the terms with her, we had a real plan, with real potential; as long as Suzy could keep herself out of depression and maintain the energy to complete her schooling over the next several years.

At our next session, Suzy walked in with a big smile on her face. I could tell something exciting had happened.

"You're looking good today, Suzy. How was your week?"

"Bracha, you won't believe this!"

"Tell me."

"I stopped a panic attack!"

"You stopped a panic attack?" I wanted to be sure I had heard right. "That is absolutely amazing! What did you do?"

"I felt it coming and started doing the *'re-laaaax'* breathing. That was enough. After a few seconds, it was gone."

"I am so proud of you! Let me give you a big hug!"

Suzy had come a really long way in a relatively short amount of time. We still worked on several other issues and then mutually decided that she could stop our sessions. She continued with the talk therapy, as her psychologist was dealing with issues that I had not touched upon. But I knew that from our work together she had received a varied range of tools to help her through the challenges she was presently encountering and others that might come up in the future. I told her to call me from time to time to let me hear how she was doing. And, I said, I wanted an invitation to her graduation when she finished her art therapy certification. I believed she was capable of reaching that happy day.

9

CELLULAR HEALING

Evelyn Cantor

Evelyn called to ask if I could help someone with a physical problem. I said it all depended on the situation. I explained to her the concept of the mind-body connection and how the mind could affect the body just as the body could affect the mind. I asked her to tell me what was bothering her.

"I am being treated for multiple sclerosis, although the doctors' diagnosis was not at all unanimous. They told me that making a definitive diagnosis is difficult because there are no specific tests for MS and symptoms vary so widely from person to person. I've been put on several medications but still suffer quite a bit.

"Can you describe your symptoms to me?"

"Fatigue, muscle spasms in my legs, stiffness and weakness, difficulty in walking, pain, and depression and anxiety."

"I'm really sorry to hear that. Why don't you come in and I'll teach you some stress-reduction techniques? That's sure to help."

She came for a session later that week. I saw before me a thin woman with a pained expression on her face. I could see the tension she was holding in her neck and shoulder muscles.

After introductions and some small talk, I began trying to unravel the reason for her excess tension.

"Can you describe to me how an average day goes by, from when you get up till you go to bed?" I asked.

"When I wake up in the morning, I never feel rested. It's hard to get out of bed because I'm in pain and full of stiffness. But I have to begin functioning and get the kids off to school. Since I have no choice, I pull myself out of bed and do the best I can. Sometimes I yell at the kids because I'm not feeling well. But what's worse is that I don't have the energy to play with them, even to show them my love. I feel I'm just too exhausted to be a real mother. When I get muscle spasms in my legs, I can't even walk. I just lie on the couch or in bed and do nothing. I'm sure that's why I feel so depressed.

"I drag through the day and feel very unfulfilled. When I go to bed at night, even though I feel exhausted, I find it hard to fall asleep and when I finally do, it's already really late and I don't get enough hours of deep sleep."

She hadn't mentioned a word about her husband. This raised a red flag for me.

"You didn't mention your husband.... He is in the picture?" I asked.

She hesitated for a moment before answering, barely above a whisper, and I found it hard to hear what she was saying. "My husband has his own issues. He has post-traumatic stress disorder, known as PTSD. It resulted from the time he served in the Israeli army during the Lebanon War in 1982. Ever since then he's been suffering with PTSD."

"What are his symptoms?"

"He has recurrent, unwanted distressing memories of traumatic events, and sometimes he seems to be reliving the traumatic event as if it were happening again. He has upsetting dreams and even nightmares; he's easily startled or frightened, always on guard for danger; he has trouble sleeping, and suffers from irritability, angry outbursts, aggressive behavior, negative thoughts about himself and others, and about life in general."

"Is he ever aggressive or abusive to you?" I needed to become aware of domestic violence or rule it out. In those cases, I refer the client on to other professionals.

"He has his angry outbursts, but I know it's not really about me. It's more about his inner turmoil. He never gets physically violent."

"That's good to know. What kind of help is he getting?"

"He sees a psychiatrist and takes medications. But they only help a little bit. We also went for marriage counseling, which was somewhat helpful."

"Do you ever think about leaving the marriage?"

"Oh no!" she was quick to answer. "I care too much about him. Also the children—I don't want to break up the family and create more problems than they have already."

"I see. So, if during our sessions together I teach you coping skills for stress and ways of feeling more positive about life in general, would you see that as an adequate outcome for you?"

"Sure. That would be great!"

"And, I believe, if you practice those skills regularly, your fatigue and pain will be reduced, maybe even substantially. Actually, a reduction in your physical symptoms would be a sign that you have reduced your stress and anxiety. This is valuable feedback for you, since stress and anxiety create inflammation in your body. Reducing inflammation is vitally important for you because MS is an autoimmune disease in which your own immune system causes inflammation that damages myelin, the fatty substance that surrounds and insulates your nerve fibers. The more stress and anxiety you have, the more inflammation in your body, which, obviously, will aggravate your MS symptoms."

"OK, great. Whatever you can teach me about managing my stress would be wonderful, because I don't feel I am in control of my stress even a little bit."

"I always teach stress-management skills to anyone suffering with a physical issue. We all have the mind-body connection, and everyone is affected by their inner feelings, whether they realize it or not."

I taught her several breathing techniques, as well as Emotional Freedom Technique,ᵛ which involves tapping on energy points along the meridians. This would be a way for her to relieve discomfort on her own, to a larger or lesser degree.

I had her wear a rubber band on her wrist and whenever she said anything negative or had a negative thought, she was instructed to pull and release the rubber band so it would snap at her wrist. This was akin to giving herself a gentle slap, reminding her to "stop that naughty behavior." Through constant repetition of this simple technique she would be able to successfully break her pattern of negative thinking.

That was the first step of this exercise and relatively simple to carry out. Not surprisingly, the next part was harder for her. After snapping the rubber band, she then had to reconstruct the thoughts or words and express them in a neutral or more positive manner. When she could not think of how to reframe a sentence we would practice together.

"Tell me, Evelyn, what would you say instead of, 'Oh, who took my car keys? I feel like exploding because I'm late for my appointment!'"

She thought long and hard. "I can't come up with anything."

"How about, 'I wonder where my car keys are. I guess Hashem wants me to be late for this appointment. I'll get there at exactly the time Hashem thinks is best for me.'"

After a while, she got used to reframing, and slowly, her negative thinking and speaking were significantly reduced. Once she could banish negative words from her mind, she could make space for positivity to fill her instead. The two opposite emotions could not reside within simultaneously. She now had to make a conscious decision and effort to choose positivity over negativity.

This was just the beginning, the foundational step, of our journey. Once negative thinking was no longer draining her energy like a vampire sucking blood, we could focus on filling her with positivity and joy. This would surely improve the quality of her life, including her debilitating MS symptoms.

I felt it was important for her to feel greater fulfillment in life. Getting up in the morning with more energy would ensure a good start to the day. This would enable her to do her tasks more quickly and give her free time for doing the things she enjoyed. We discussed in detail the activities she considered fun and invigorating. I wanted her to clearly know that a positive change in her life could become her new reality. In order to accomplish these goals, I created a visualization especially for her. Since I had never used this visualization before, I was curious as to its outcome.

After putting her into a light trance, I had her imagine waking up in the morning.

"Feel yourself in bed, with your eyes still closed.... Maybe you yawn or stretch...as you become more wide awake.... Now, before getting up, you say *modeh ani*...thanking Hashem for returning your soul to you.... As you say the words, concentrate on your feelings of gratitude.... Thank Hashem for giving you another day of life...another day of opportunity.... Do that now."

After a pause, I continued.

"The more gratitude you express to Hashem...the more opportunities He will give you...to feel gratitude.... He will send you His messengers...to enable you to experience more and more situations...in your daily life...that you can be grateful for.... It's a law Hashem has set up in the world....What you give out comes back to you...."

I was silent for a long pause to let the message sink in.

"Evelyn, now tell yourself that today...will be a good day...a happy day...and you will do something of value in this day.... As you lie in bed...still not getting up...breathe deeply and slowly...doing the *'re-laaaax'* breathing I taught you....

"Imagine a big helium balloon with a string attached floating toward you.... You notice that the string is held...by a spiritual being.... You notice the color of that balloon.... What color is it?"

She tells me.

"The *malach* of happiness is bringing you the balloon.... Written on it in big black letters...are the words 'Happy Monday' or 'Tuesday' or whatever day it is.... You feel the *malach* of happiness...tying the string of the balloon to your wrist.... You can feel some of that happiness flowing into your body.... As you lie there, you feel an upward pull on your arm.... The balloon is calling you...to take part in a happy day....

"Then another helium balloon with a string attached...is being brought toward you.... Another spiritual being...is approaching with it.... This is the *malach* of laughter.... What color is this balloon?"

I waited for her answer.

"The balloon has written on it 'Laughter is the best medicine!'.... The *malach* of laughter...is tying the string of the balloon to your wrist.... You feel a bubble of laughter welling up inside of you.... It's a great feeling.... You become aware of a stronger tug on your arm...as you lie there."

I continued with the visualization in which several more balloons were attached to her other wrist and shoulders. Each had an encouraging title, such as 'energy,' 'pride,' 'protected and safe,' and so on. I noticed a smile replacing her former morose expression.

I then had her imagine a vibrant energy within the balloons pulling her up and out of bed. She saw herself washing *netilas yadayim* and beginning her morning routine.

"Those balloons are staying with you....Allow them to pull you into the kitchen.... Your movements are fluid and effortless...you feel invigorated and eager to start your day.... You look forward to greeting your children...happily and energetically.... You happily and energetically prepare breakfast...with a feeling of pride in your efforts...."

I had her visualize each action involved in preparing breakfast and how she interacted very positively with her children. I told her to feel great pride in all that she was doing. And once the children had left for school, the balloons left as well. I had her visualize spending some time doing a fun activity, one that gave her pleasure. I also gave her the option of giving herself a tasty treat.

I purposely left her husband out of the visualization. I did not wish any negative associations to mar her transformative process.

However, I had included a balloon giving her the feelings of protection and safety, just in case she imagined him entering the scene uninvited. I strongly believed that all that we were doing would have the added benefit of enabling her to live more comfortably with him.

I continued with the visualization. "Now that you know...you can start off your day...happily and energetically...and that you can be happy and energetic...with your children...and even have a little laugh with them...you know that you can continue doing this...on a daily basis....

"I want you to know that...every morning after you say *modeh ani*...the *malachim* will come and bring you...the balloons as they have now.... The balloons will pull you forward...with energy and motivation.... Each morning all you do...is say *modeh ani*...and the *malachim* will come to you...one by one, and tie their balloons to your wrists and shoulders.... This is a gift you will receive...each morning...and it will help you begin your day...with happiness and energy.... Every morning...you will wait for the *malachim*...to bring you their balloons before getting up.... You simply say the words '*modeh ani*'...and they will start to come...with their gifts to you....

"You can also say *modeh ani* at other times...not only in the morning.... Saying *modeh ani* will act as a switch...just like a light switch...that will turn on your memory...of seeing the *malachim* coming...with their balloons.... Whenever you want the *malachim*...to come with their balloons...with their gifts to you...just say the words '*modeh ani*'...and you flipped the switch on...and then they will come."

I repeated the message numerous times in various forms because repetition makes the suggestion stick. At the same time, I was creating a "post-hypnotic suggestion," something she would unconsciously do or experience in her daily life as a result of the suggestions she had received while in hypnosis. I wanted her to become empowered by being able to create within herself happiness and energy and any of those other positive emotions the balloons gave her whenever she wished. The post-hypnotic suggestion would cause her to automatically, without conscious thought, imagine the balloons being attached to her body every time she said the words 'modeh ani,' and she would thereby experience the magical transformation they created.

Once she came out of trance, I helped her figure out a menu of several healthy treats. Rewarding herself with a tasty prize would be a way to bolster her sense of pride in the positive changes she was making.

After three sessions, I noted a marked change in her demeanor. She looked and felt much better. Her facial skin color let me know that her health was improving.

"I feel so much lighter!" Evelyn's voice had an energetic ring to it. "It's like I always had this heaviness dragging me down, making it so hard to move and to do anything. And now it feels so different!"

"Isn't that wonderful, Evelyn!" I was so pleased that her efforts were paying off.

"Maybe those balloons really are pulling me along!" she added laughingly.

"Who can gage just how powerful the mind is? It certainly appears to be 'mind over matter.' And how are the pain and stiffness?"

"Better, maybe 30 to 40 percent better."

"Great! That's a wonderful improvement." I knew that her feeling happier and more fulfilled would positively alter her perception of pain.

"What about the leg spasms and your difficulty with walking?"

"They're bothering me a lot."

"I'm sorry to hear that. Please, tell me more. How strong are the spasms? Are they the same in both legs? How often do you have them? Do they affect your walking? Tell me whatever you can about what's going on."

Evelyn let forth a huge sigh. She became visibly upset.

"It's my left leg much more that the right one. Sometimes the pain is so bad that I can't walk. The muscle must be atrophied because even when I walk, I have a severe limp and the leg looks emaciated."

"Yes, I noticed that. What do you do to make the spasm go away?"

"I take a muscle relaxant."

"How long does it take for the muscle to relax?"

"It varies. Sometimes I feel better in half an hour and sometimes it takes a few hours. I take pain meds when the spasm doesn't pass."

"Do you know of any reason why the spasm doesn't pass quickly after taking the muscle relaxant like it does other times? Are you in a different setting? Are you under more stress? Think about what might be different in those situations. Close your eyes and try to remember a time when the spasm was so bad that it didn't want to go away. Imagine the scene as it happened then." I always want to discover if there are any reasons other than physical ones that make a condition worse.

Evelyn sat quietly with her eyes closed for about two minutes. Suddenly her eyes popped open.

"Yes," she exclaimed, "I remember! I was getting out of the elevator and very nervous that maybe my neighbors were standing in the hall talking, as they often do, and they would watch me limp to my apartment. Sure enough, when the doors of the elevator opened, I saw them there and I felt so ashamed as they looked at me, not saying anything but pitying me in their hearts. The spasm started right there in the hallway. When I finally got into the house, it was so bad, I had to take a double dose of medication for it to go away. Now that I think of it, every time I'm in the elevator I get this nervous feeling and the spasm starts up. When the neighbors are not in the hall watching me, the spasm passes faster. I didn't realize it till now."

"I'm glad you're able to realize this very important fact. When you are anxious your physical symptoms will be worse. Do you agree?"

"It does seem to be so."

"So we will find a way to reduce your anxiety when you believe that people are watching you walk, or even when you just fear that they might turn up and begin watching you."

"I can't help my feelings, you know," she retorted defensively.

"I'm not blaming you or criticizing you," I said gently. "I'm simply stating what seems to be an important factor in the way you experience your symptoms. If you do have this anxiety, let's see what we can do to eliminate it."

"I don't see what you can do to make me feel more relaxed. I dread getting out of the elevator!"

"Does it happen to you in other situations when people are around?" I wanted to know.

After a moment of reflection, she replied. "If it's my family or close friends who I talk to about my condition, it doesn't make a difference. It happens with people that I don't know or am not close to who will pity me when they see me limping like that."

"You know, Evelyn, if you won't pity yourself, others won't either. And if you do the best you can under the circumstances, then that is definitely a reason to be proud of yourself. If you will be proud of yourself, others will be too."

I was giving her empowering suggestions that would help her let go of obsessing about what others were thinking of her.

"How can I be proud of myself if these legs do such a miserable job of carrying me around?" I could hear the angry frustration bursting out of her words. She began crying. I gave her some tissues and told her to do the slow *re-laaaax* breathing. When she was calmer, I felt we could start doing therapeutic work.

I began talking in my slow hypnotic voice to induce trance indirectly. "Evelyn, just as you never believed...the 'balloons' could give you more energy...and get you to move more effortlessly...you may not believe...but yet be pleasantly surprised...with what we can do...about your leg spasms...."

"Your legs are your loyal servants.... For how many years...have they been carrying you around?.... When was the last time you felt grateful...for having a right leg...or a left leg?.... When was the last time...you said thank you for having them?"

She looked at me with wide open eyes, not speaking, just absorbing my words.

"I want you to try and remember now...think back...to a time when...."

Her eyes closed without my asking her to do so.

"...you last spoke...either to your right leg or your left leg.... What did you tell it?.... Going deeper now...deeper and deeper...with every breath you take.... Moving back through all the years of your life.... Did you ever thank Hashem in appreciation for your right leg...or your left leg...for working so loyally for you...for so many years...without pay...without reward?.... Or did you express anger that they were in spasm...that they were limping...through no fault of their own?.... How many years did your legs...serve you faithfully...perfectly...without...any hesitation...any difficulty?.... Tell me...how long?"

She mumbled, "Forty years."

"Did you once say thank you to Hashem for your legs?.... Did you ever express appreciation to them?"

"Never."

"How do you feel when you work tirelessly...for others and no one...says thank you?.... If your legs had feelings...maybe they would be feeling sad...that you never tell them a good word...that you never thank Hashem for giving them to you.... If they had feelings...might they be starved...for a word of gratitude?.... Could that be?"

She nodded.

"From this day onward...you will have a new relationship with your legs.... You will begin expressing gratitude...appreciation...love...for your wonderful, loyal legs...that are working for you...for so many years...perhaps without ever hearing one kind word from you.... And now they are struggling...with a debilitating health condition...to continue to serve you faithfully....Do you think you can do that?"

I reiterated, in several different ways, the need to express gratitude to Hashem for the legs He had given her. Rav Yisroel Zev Gustman,[vi] out of gratitude that his life was saved by hiding in a forest and eating of its plants during the Holocaust, personally acted as a gardener watering the shrubbery in his yeshiva in Israel. Gratitude is a powerful force.

Additionally, Evelyn's newly felt appreciation would create a feeling of love for her legs. Appreciation, praise, and love directed toward her suffering legs would act as water poured onto a parched piece of land. It is only natural that the land becomes more productive when it receives what it sorely lacks. When we feel love and gratitude for someone, the positive energy produced creates a positive change in them. We see this with plants that are spoken to, have music played to them, or are touched gently—their growth is stimulated as a result.

Obviously, her legs could only function as Hashem enabled them to; they had no independent power. But by sending out positive energy to them, she could most likely improve their function. She was now learning to appreciate and love them as being the limbs Hashem had given her to serve her, and to express those feelings in concrete ways.

"From now on...every day...you will thank Hashem for your legs.... You will thank Hashem that your legs know how to function.... Each of your legs is a *shaliach* of Hashem...a servant of Hashem...serving you...in the way Hashem created it to.... You can have a dialogue with them....Every day you will tell them in your own words...how much you appreciate...everything they are doing for you...as messengers of Hashem...carrying you around...doing the best they can for you....

"And then, you will show your legs...especially the left one...which is suffering more than the right one...how much you love them, how much you care...how much you appreciate what they are doing for you.... Are you willing to do this?"

She nodded.

"When your leg or legs hurt...when one or both are in spasm...you will take some oil...arnica oil...or lavender oil...and massage each one...lovingly...telling your legs...how happy you are that Hashem has given them to you...and how much you care for them...and how much you appreciate...how much you thank them...because you realize that they are messengers of Hashem...doing Hashem's will to serve you.... You realize how hard they are working for you...despite the situation…doing the best they can for you…. You massage each leg until it relaxes and feels better…. You continue massaging…and thanking and praising them…until the spasm is gone…. Are you willing to do that?"

Again, she nodded.

"Please tell me…in your own words…what you plan to do for your precious legs and what you will say to them."

It took her some time, but she did put together a few sentences that conveyed her newfound feelings. The anger she had previously expressed toward her legs was gone, replaced by the positive emotions I had worked at implanting in her mind.

Subsequent to our session, Evelyn began a daily routine of massaging her legs with aromatherapy oils and talking to them appreciatively and lovingly. She reported, with great surprise, that she had immediately felt improvement in the degree and frequency of the spasms. I was mildly surprised but knew from experience that physical healing of all sorts, including cellular healing, could easily come about through working with the mind-body connection.

I was aware that MS symptoms can lessen and even disappear for a while, that there are remissions and relapses with the disease. I was hoping that the work we were doing, which certainly was able to reduce inflammation, would enable her to feel relief from her symptoms for a lengthy period of time.

I encouraged Evelyn to continue daily massage of her legs and gradually over time decrease the massaging to once or twice a week. At some point she reported to me that the spasms were becoming quite rare. When she did experience a flare-up, she immediately took care of her legs with the "gratitude-love-therapy" I had taught her. She even said that her left leg was looking healthier than it did before. I suspected that the increased blood flow, as a result of the massage, was at the root of that change. But certainly, Evelyn's improvement strengthened my belief that one should never leave out the ingredients of peace, joy, gratitude, and love as parts of a healing tonic.

I continued our therapy with several sessions of enhancing Evelyn's self-esteem and self-love. This was vitally important for her well-being, especially since she could not rely on her husband for emotional support. As a result of the work we did, her self-consciousness in the presence of others was greatly decreased. It did not take long before Evelyn was walking with much more confidence and stability than she had in a very long time. This she was soon able to do, without batting an eyelid, even when the neighbors were standing around in the hallway.

Lilly Jacobs

Lilly's problem was high blood pressure. She suspected it was related to stress as it fluctuated with the goings-on in her life. After she bought a blood-pressure monitor and checked her numbers daily, she easily noticed the relationship between her stress and elevated readings. She wanted to learn to control her blood pressure before her doctor would insist on giving her medication.

Sometimes people create their own stress by poor lifestyle habits, such as maintaining unhealthy relationships or creating unnecessary debt. But this was not the case with Lilly. A widow, with three young children to raise, she often was buffeted by the stormy winds of her difficult existence, totally outside of her control. She understood the concept of mind-body healing and was eager to implement stress-management techniques in order to alleviate her hypertension.

As with all clients suffering from a physical ailment, I taught Lilly breathing exercises and recorded a relaxation trance for her to listen to at home.

"Deep relaxation is crucial for releasing tension," I explained. "If you can listen to the recording twice a day, it will greatly benefit your nervous system."

"I'm not sure if I can find the time to listen twice a day," Lilly replied, "but I definitely will work it into my schedule. I think I'd love to listen to it in bed at night. It will help me fall into a deep, relaxing sleep."

"Good. This is the foundation of my program for you. If you practice the breathing exercises twice a day and listen to the recording at least once a day, it will help, but it might not be enough. Next time, we'll go deeper. Let me know during the week how you feel."

At our session the following week, she reported that sometimes her blood pressure was stable but, as I suspected, if she had undergone a particularly difficult experience it would jump up by several numbers.

"I'm glad you have seen some positive results," I said. "I want you to continue doing these exercises as they will be more and more beneficial for all your systems over time. But today we'll do something additional, called 'cellular healing.' This will actually affect your cells and bring about real, lasting change in your cardiovascular system. Would you like that?"

"I surely would," was her enthusiastic response. "How do you do that?"

"By doing a simple visualization in which you adjust your blood pressure to the desired amount."

The quizzical expression on Lilly's face made me smile. She wasn't my first client to be skeptical of the power of the mind to heal the body.

"Nothing is foolproof, but these techniques usually work. Scientific research has come up with the evidence. If you wish to know more you can check out the work of the legendary Dr. Milton Erickson,[vii] a psychiatrist specializing in medical hypnosis. His research has proven that your thoughts have a direct effect on your health. And there's Dr. Candace Pert,[viii] Dr. Carl Simonton,[ix] Dr. Bernie Siegal,[x] and…shall I give you more names?"

"No, no, I believe you!" she said, while shaking her head vigorously.

"All right, enough said. How about if we begin?"

"I trust you know what you are doing."

"I have worked this way many times in the past with excellent results. My goal is to do what is best for you. If your subconscious mind does not agree with my assessment of how to proceed, we won't. I can't make you do anything your subconscious mind is opposed to. In general, I rarely tell you what to do. I guide you so that you realize yourself what needs to be done. If you feel uncomfortable with anything I am saying, just tell me. This is your journey, not mine. We move forward in the way that feels good for you and at your pace. Some people move ahead quickly and some slowly. It's up to you.

"Sure. I'm OK with it. I do want to do this. And I trust you."

"Thank you. I appreciate that you are putting your trust in me.... So, now make yourself comfortable in the chair...."

I took my time putting her into a deep trance. What we were going to do was, in my eyes, one of the most amazing aspects of hypnosis, healing the body by using the mind.

"I'd like you to see yourself now...as two 'Lillys'...two of you....One Lilly is resting in the armchair...and the other Lilly is observing you resting so comfortably.... The 'you' in the armchair appears to be sleeping.... She feels so comfortable, so relaxed.... You, Lilly, standing next to the armchair...are soon to go on a healing journey.... You will not be alone.... My voice will go with you...on this amazing journey.... Do you feel ready to embark on this healing journey?"

I paused and noticed a slight nod of her head.

"As you stand there...next to yourself resting in the recliner...as you continue looking at yourself...imagine that you are becoming smaller and smaller...and smaller...until you are so small...that you can easily enter an opening in Lilly's body, the one who is resting.... I will give you a moment now...to make yourself so small...that you can easily enter Lilly's body through some opening....

"You are so small now...and you enter an opening...and find yourself inside your body.... It is dark inside...and you have a strong flashlight...that lights the way for you.... Your feet begin to walk...you don't know where they are taking you...but your feet take you where your subconscious mind...is telling them to go.... Your way is lighted by the flashlight...and you are curious to know...where you are going....

"You stop in front of a room...On the door of the room, written in big bold letters...are the words...'Control Room of the Brain'.... You know you are meant to enter...but before you do...send a *tefillah* to Hashem to help you...do some good...accomplish something useful...something positive.... Send that *tefillah* to Hashem now...."

I waited long enough for her to do that.

"Now take hold of the handle and open the door.... You enter this room.... It is a gigantic room with many machines, gadgets, and computers.... You look to the right and to the left...in front and in the back and up and down.... It is like a gigantic factory with so many different machines...and gadgets working.... Listen to the noise of wheels turning...pumps pumping...whirring sounds...knocking sounds...clanging sounds...bumping sounds....

"The brain controls all the systems of the body.... Each machine and computer...has a sign on it...immune system...endocrine system...digestive system.... You scan the room...looking for your circulatory system...looking to the right...the left...front and back.... After a while you spot it...the machine that says 'Cardiovascular System.'.... You approach and come close...to see how it works....

"There is a gauge with numbers from 1 to 100.... You realize that the middle numbers...from 40 to 60 are the normal range of blood pressure...the numbers below 40 are low blood pressure...and the numbers above 60 are high blood pressure.... There is a dial attached to this gauge...and there is a pointer...that points to the number...of your blood pressure right now.... You can turn the dial and the pointer will move.... To which number is the pointer pointing now?"

She told me.

"You know that is higher than what is best for you.... You know that you can turn the dial...and the pointer will move...either to higher numbers...or to lower numbers.... Your inner wisdom tells you...which number is best for your health.... Turn the dial now...so that the pointer points...to that number of blood pressure...that your inner mind tells you is best for you.... Do that now...."

I paused while she imagined turning the dial.

"Does the pointer remain in place?.... Or does it jump back to the previous number?.... You can keep the dial in place...in case it moves...by gluing it...or screwing it in...or taping it.... Just tight enough for now...just in case there is an important reason...for your circulatory system...to raise or lower your blood pressure...it will be able to do so.... So just lightly fix the dial in place for now.... Let me know...with a nod of your head...when the dial remains in place...at the number you wish to keep it at."

I waited for her head nod.

"Good.... Excellent.... You will come back here...every time you undergo...a disturbing incident...and check to see...if your numbers are right...right for you and best for your health.... If you need to...you will adjust the dial again...just as you have done now.... You may tell your cardiovascular system...one of Hashem's messengers...implanted in your body...that you will do your part...in keeping your blood pressure stable...by practicing deep breathing and relaxation....Now you ask Hashem to please...enable it...your cardiovascular system...to do its part as well in keeping you healthy.... Thank your cardiovascular system for being a loyal servant of Hashem...in working for you...all these years...in maintaining a blood flow...and keeping you alive....

"And now it is time to leave.... You exit the room and close the door behind you.... Spend a moment thanking Hashem...for this amazing opportunity...to do something for your health...and for your ability to maintain a healthy blood pressure level....

"Going back out...of your body...the way you came in...exiting from that opening...that let you in.... Stand next to yourself reclining in the recliner.... Return to your full size...as you were before.... Look at yourself...how relaxed and at peace you appear...in the recliner....

"And now...merging with yourself...in the recliner...so that the two of you are one again.... And all that you have learned and experienced...is now incorporated deeply into the sleeping Lilly.... Knowing that whenever you have the need...to adjust your blood pressure...you can do so with ease...by simply closing your eyes...and taking a few deep breaths.... You will exhale slowly...and feel the tension leave your muscles and your blood vessels.... With each exhale...you release the tension more and more...as your blood pressure eases into the normal, healthy range.... And when you wish to keep those healthy levels in place...you can easily go within your body...to your Control Room of the Brain...and make the adjustments there as necessary....

"And when you have finished absorbing...all of that wonderful new knowledge...into the deepest part of your being...then...and only then...will you slowly...gradually...effortlessly...become awake and alert...coming to full consciousness...feeling better...and happier...than you have felt...in a very long time."

It took Lilly a long time to come fully out of trance. When she did, she looked at me with tears in her eyes.

"How do you feel?" I asked.

"Wonderful! Hopeful.... It seems so simple. I wonder if it really is."

"It depends a lot on you. If you think it will be simple, most likely it will be. And if you think it will be complicated, then most likely it will be complicated. We create our reality to a large degree by what we think and believe. So be careful with what you think and say, and train yourself to be as positive as you can. It can only help you in so many different ways.

"You have seen in this past week that you have had some success in lowering your blood pressure. Now you have another powerful tool to add to your regime. With Hashem's help, you'll see wonderful results.

"I made a recording of your journey to the Control Room. Use it as often as you wish. After a while, you will be able to do the visualization without the recording, as it will become second nature to you. Call me to let me know how things are progressing and if you wish to set up another appointment."

Lilly thanked me profusely for helping her in only two sessions. She called later that week saying that she was listening regularly to the Control Room tape and felt no need for another appointment at this point.

After several weeks, she called to say that her blood pressure was stable and in the healthy range. And, she said, she had become so acutely attuned to her body that she could tell when her blood pressure became elevated. Then she would do her exercises very regularly and, within a short time, could feel her blood pressure going back to normal.

Lilly's amazing success was one of many that I experienced with cellular-healing techniques. The "Control Room of the Brain" was a place I visited on many occasions. Once again, I realized, so vividly, that "mind over matter" is not a myth.

10

CANCER

Naomi Stein

She never believed she could be helped. I had to convince her that it paid to try, and that she had nothing to lose since I wasn't going to charge her for my services. I felt such compassion and I so wanted to change her fate, even slightly, if I possibly could.

My dear friend Naomi Stein had pancreatic cancer and was being treated by one of the most prestigious doctors for that particular cancer in Memorial Sloan Kettering Cancer Center,[xi] one of the best cancer hospitals in the world, located in New York City. But Naomi was broken. She had no faith in the medical system and despised every aspect of her treatment. She hated the chemotherapy, she hated the hospital, and she even hated her doctor. I knew if Naomi was to heal, she had to get out of her negative mindset.

Right after returning from Boston, where I had taken an advanced hypno-oncology course, I immediately contacted her. I planned on staying with my niece for a few days before going home to Israel, and I wanted to make the most out of my visit to Brooklyn by working with Naomi who lived nearby. I told her that I needed to implement what I had just learned, and asked her, almost as a favor, if she would agree to my practicing on her. She didn't have much faith in the healing capabilities of hypnosis, but she readily agreed to "help me out."

I met with Naomi daily for several hours for the next five days. My main goal was getting Naomi to see the treatments as a gift rather than the poisons she felt they were.

"Naomi," I asked in all sincerity, "do you have any option for treatment other than doing what you're now doing?"

"No," she answered despondently. "I wanted to do alternative healing, but my husband asked our *rav*, and he said we should go to the best doctor for pancreatic cancer and take advantage of her years of experience and the most advanced scientific discoveries. Since she has treated thousands of patients and even patented a device that delivers the chemo straight to the affected organ, rather than circulating throughout the body, we decided to go to her. She's considered top in her field, and we have the *rav*'s *berachah*. So I should feel OK with the treatments. But I don't. I literally hate what's going on!"

"Tell me what you hate about it."

"Well for one thing, I believe chemotherapy is poison. I feel as though I'm putting bleach and ammonia into my body."

I wrote that down.

"What else do you hate?"

She introspected for a minute, trying to discover what exactly she hated. Finally, she said, "Every time I get close to the hospital and see the words SLOAN KETTERING CANCER CENTER on the building, all of my insides cringe. Already, still in the street, I can smell the antiseptic hospital smells, I'm imagining sitting in the recliner being hooked up to the chemo, and I shudder. Just seeing the building and the 'C' word triggers all of that." She closed her eyes, and I could see she was reliving some distressful situation.

"Anything else?" I persevered.

"Oh yes! That doctor is really a robot instead of a human being. She treats sixty people one after the other, and allows a maximum of ten minutes with each patient, mostly just five minutes. She has no time for explaining things or answering questions. She lets her assistants do that. She comes in, looks at the chart, asks one or two questions, and writes her instructions down for the nurse or the intern to follow. There's absolutely no personal interaction. I'm just a room number to her."

"My gosh! That's a lot to deal with!"

My empathetic comment was a pitiful attempt at alleviating her pain. I could clearly see why she felt so miserable about her situation. We had a lot of work cut out for us. I still did not know exactly what to do. But one thing I did know; I'd have to reframe all of Naomi's beliefs and attitudes about her treatment and anyone and anything involved with it. When creating effective sessions, I rely on my intuition rather than any fixed formulas for conducting hypnosis. I consider this intuition a gift from Hashem, and *b'siyata d'Shmaya*, it rarely fails me. I fervently davened that Hashem should now give me the guidance to know how best to devise Naomi's therapy.

I took my time putting Naomi into a deeply relaxed state and bringing her to a safe and beautiful place. When I could tell that she was in a deep trance, I put her through a scenario intended to make her think she was in one place, but would soon come to realize that it was, in fact, a different place entirely.

She saw a building and the sign on the door read "Butcher Shop." She saw and smelled a shop that cut up and sold meat and fowl. She was sure that that's where she was. She didn't like this place, the sights, the smells, the sounds. Then, guiding her through a lengthy visualization, I had her discover that this place was really only a front for an entirely different activity. In this establishment they prepared meats for desperately poor people, which were given to them for free, anonymously. That was their entire raison d'être, but in order to be able to afford their acts of kindness, they sold meat to their paying customers. So, far from being a place that chopped up flesh and sold it to put money in the owner's pocket, it was really a place that cared so deeply about unfortunates, that everything they did, although appearing rough and for personal profit, was actually done out of love for humanity. They even hid their charitable acts from the public so that the recipients of their kindness could not figure out where they were getting their gifts of food from.

This butcher shop was merely a metaphor. As I continued my hypnotic suggestions, she soon came to believe that the hospital she so hated—cutting up flesh and acting out of self-interest—was really a lofty institution of kindness. The details between the metaphor and its meaning did not have to match exactly, as long as she now believed that the hospital was really a place quite different than what she had imagined it to be previously, just as the butcher shop was. She now saw it as an institution that performed acts of kindness, no matter how "gross" those acts appeared outwardly. Now, when she saw the words "MEMORIAL SLOAN KETTERING CANCER CENTER" on the building, she became filled with a feeling of pride for this lofty institution, and even a certain joy in being involved with it. Although those feelings were not totally rational, I knew that if she felt very positively toward the locale of her treatments, anticipating something good happening to her there, those feelings would greatly enhance her chances of healing.

That was our first session. She was back the next day.

"So, how are you feeling today about Sloan Kettering?" I asked Naomi after she settled herself comfortably in the recliner. I knew she had been there the afternoon after our session.

"I don't understand it!" she said. "It's like it's not the same place. I feel so different about it, so positive, that it just doesn't make sense. How can it be?"

"It's not the same place!" I said emphatically. "Your previous perceptions made it into a place of horror for you, something like a butcher house. Your new perceptions, the true perceptions, make it into a place of healing for you and others. And that is your new reality. To a certain degree, we create our reality.

"Amazing! The power of the mind!"

"How true."

My goal for today's session was to reframe her attitude about her medications. Her belief that she was allowing bleach and ammonia to be put inside her body would only harm her and never enable the medications to heal her. If a placebo, an ineffective sugar pill, could heal in as much as 35 percent of the cases it is used, because the recipient believes it is a powerful drug, then her chemo could possibly heal her if she believed in its ability to do so. With the power of the mind, I could perhaps get Naomi to believe that the chemotherapy had the ability to heal and was actually doing so for her.

In trance, I used a similar technique as I had used the day before to change Naomi's perception of her drugs. In an altered state of consciousness, instead of seeing a colorless bleach and ammonia solution, I had her see a liquid I called "sparkling mineral water." This, I explained, was a product Hashem had designed and given over to His agents of healing, the doctors who were now treating her. I lauded the benefits of this "sparkling tonic." I knew that in truth, it didn't necessarily matter whether the liquid was truly healing, as long as she believed that there was a good chance of success. In this way, her belief in the drugs she had so hated previously could now turn into a source of healing for her.

"As the 'sparkling mineral water'...Hashem's miraculous tonic...enters your body," I intoned, "you can feel it moving through your cells...of your pancreas...and all of your cells.... The 'sparkling mineral waters' cleanse...purify...revitalize...regenerate and...*heal!*.... Feel the effects...of this amazing tonic in your body...Feel the gentle pulsation...of healing energy.... Feel the healing vibrations...in your body now."

When she let me know that she could feel this positive energy circulating in the cells of her pancreas and throughout her body, I was satisfied that her next treatment would be a totally transformed experience.

I continued to enhance the effects of her new perception.

"The 'sparkling mineral water' is also...feeding and nurturing the white cells...of your immune system.... See now those wondrous white T cells...imagine them in any way you wish.... They are given to you by Hashem...to serve as a protective force within your body....

See them now multiplying...and multiplying...until they form a vast army of white warriors...ready and able to protect your body...from any invading enemy agents.... Let me know when you see that vast army in front of you.... Let me know how those white warriors...appear to you."

I had her describe to me how she imagined her newly empowered white soldiers and how, in great detail, they were going to eradicate the foe.

"See now your vast army of white soldiers...dedicated and loyal to you...to protect you in the best way possible...see them now going forth...and clearing out that which needs to be cleared out...of your body.... See them doing their job...Hashem created this white army for...cleansing and clearing and cleaning out...that which does not belong inside of you...for your health and well-being.... Watch and enjoy the scenes of victory taking place now."

I paused long enough for her to her imagine, in whichever way she chose, her immune system restoring her body to health, free of the growth that threatened her life. Her face took on a joyful glow.

"Please tell me, Naomi...what you think about the 'sparkling tonic'...the 'sparkling mineral water'...that Hashem's messengers are giving you for your healing.... How do you feel as it enters your body?"

I wanted her to hear herself express in words what she now believed about the chemotherapy treatment. If she could believe that it was acting as a powerful catalyst for healing, it would have the ability to be that for her. If she still had negative beliefs about the chemo, it would be quite unlikely to heal her. Her belief in the efficacy of the drugs was more important than the actual abilities they possessed. Her belief in her survival was, according to modern science, the greatest contributing factor to her actual survival.

"I'm happy...that Hashem's messengers...have the 'sparkling tonic'...that can heal me.... I'm so grateful that they are giving it to me."

This was exactly what I wished to hear. She had expressed, on her own, what she now felt about her chemotherapy treatments. This was tremendous progress.

Upon her return the following day, I was encouraged by Naomi's positivity and changed attitude toward the hospital and medications. However, she still harbored resentment toward her main caretaker, Dr. Sabrina Ziegler, for her robotic interactions with her patients. I knew she was due for a hospital visit the following day for treatment. If I could change my friend's perception toward her doctor before she met her, I believed that the 'healing tonic' she would be given might indeed be healing.

Dr. Ziegler had practiced as an oncologist for forty-four years, was world-famous, and had treated thousands of patients for pancreatic cancer across the globe. Naomi should have been happy to be in such capable hands, but I quite understood her distress with the impersonal nature of the relationship.

"Now, tell me, what kind of doctor would you like to have?" I asked.

"That's an easy question to answer," she said, with emotion. "First of all, I need to know that she cares about me as a person, not as a room number or a statistic. I'm not an addition or a deletion to her list of success stories! She never asks how I feel, just looks at the lab results in the chart. I feel like I'm just another mouse she's experimenting on in her clinic. Is that what being a doctor is all about? I thought they entered this profession because they cared about helping humanity and cared about us as individuals!"

I deeply felt for Naomi, but now was not the time to ruminate over her feelings. I needed more input from her so I could develop a plan for the hypnotic suggestions I intended to implant in her mind. In our limited time together, I wanted to be able to deliver the maximum amount of healing protocol.

"I understand," I said rather formally. "Tell me more of what you want and need from your doctor."

"I want her to call me by my first name so I get the feeling that she realizes I am a person, unique from anyone else, with a life to live."

"OK. What else?"

"I need to be able to ask her questions and get answers from her and not be told that the nurse will explain everything to me. She needs to have time, at least a few minutes, so that I can talk to her."

"Good. Makes sense. Anything else?" I was making a list as she spoke.

She sat thinking. "I want to know that she's human, with human emotions, and that if, *chas v'shalom*, I died, she would shed a tear, if not outwardly then at least on the inside." She let out a pensive sigh.

I had to rein in my feelings as Naomi spoke about the possibility of her dying, but did give her an empathetic smile. A plan for the session was gelling in my mind.

"Good!" I expressed satisfaction with what Naomi had divulged to me. "That's a lot of good input, and you can add to this list of wants and needs whenever you wish," I said, as I held the paper up in the air.

Naomi settled back more comfortably in the armchair, looking at me expectantly.

"Now, tell me more about Dr. Sabrina Ziegler and how she operates. How can she possibly treat sixty patients in one day? How many hours a day does she work?"

"The ward I'm in is set up with the nurses' station in the center, and sixty small cubicles surrounding it in a large circle. She simply goes from one to the next with an attending physician or a nurse, or student doctors, checking the charts and giving her instructions verbally and then writing them down so that there are no mistakes. Once in a while, someone asks a question and, being the *Yekke* that she is, she repeats herself and makes sure they understood her perfectly. The visit can be as short as three minutes, maximum ten. I know for a fact that she can work twelve or more hours straight. She also performs surgery and conducts research."

"OK," I rubbed my forehead as I contemplated this lady's workload. I wondered how many days a week she did this, and asked Naomi if she knew.

"I'm told she's at the hospital five days a week. She probably sleeps the entire weekend."

"I think you told me that she patented some invention. Can you tell me about it?"

"Sure. She invented a pump that is attached to a port in the abdominal area and it delivers the chemo directly to the affected organ, such as the pancreas, liver, or stomach. This way the medications have maximum impact on the cancer and are less destructive to the rest of the body. I think she was nominated for a Nobel Prize because of it. They use it in many hospitals worldwide."

"Good!" I said. I had plenty of material now for a very powerful session. I davened that Hashem would enable me to attain the most effective results possible. With Divine guidance, I knew it could happen.

"Take a deep breath now, and make yourself as comfortable as you can in the chair...."

I continued with the induction, nudging Naomi deeper and deeper into hypnosis. I performed some tests in order to gauge the depth of her trance. When I felt she was at a fairly deep level, I began the therapeutic work.

"I understand, Naomi, that you wish you had a physician that cares about you...calling you by your first name...asking how you feel, making time to answer your questions...who would care deeply if anything happened to you.... I'm sure every patient wishes for such a loving, caring, human doctor....

"Well, I have a surprise for you today.... Dr. Sabrina is really all of that.... Her name is Dr. Sabrina, because she is a human being with a unique personality...that only a 'Sabrina' has...and a unique mission in life that only a doctor has.... She really is the ideal doctor...packaged in a different way than you imagined.... Unfortunately, she has to hide those caring behaviors from you.... If she would reveal to every patient how much she cares and would spend time with them with their questions...questions that others could answer for her...she would only be able to treat a fraction...of all the sick people she wishes to help.... Because she cares so much...she wishes to help as many cancer patients as she possibly can....

"She is in such a dilemma…wanting to show you her true feelings… making the patient feel good emotionally…yet knowing that to do so would mean…that she would have so much less time to help the myriad patients…that enter Sloan Kettering…longing for a cure…. She has to decide whether or not to help four or five times as many people…without expressing emotion…or help a fraction of her patient load…by acting more human and less robotic…. What would you do in that situation? "

I let her ponder the question internally, allowing her time to absorb the true dimensions of the dilemma this amazing doctor was actually facing. After being silent a sufficient amount of time for the suggestions to gel in Naomi's mind, I continued to strengthen the point.

"Dr. Sabrina is so dedicated to her patients…that she barely allows herself time to eat or sleep…. Does she have a family, I wonder?…. Does she have any time to spend with them, I wonder? Maybe she never had children and so she pours her love into her patients…. Maybe she never married so that she would be free…to spend all her time on healing her patients….

"I think that at night before she goes to sleep…she must pray for each of her patients by name…. Since she is sacrificing so much for them…she surely wants them to heal…. Otherwise she would never continue at this pace for so many years…. If she didn't care deeply about healing, she could never physically do this!"

I spoke slowly, emphasizing every word. *"It is only because she cares so much…that she ignores her own needs…and the pleasures of life…and pushes herself to the limit…just so that she can heal another person…."*

Of course, I had no idea if my hypothesis was correct or not, but as long as Naomi believed it to be true, her attitude toward her caretaker would dramatically improve. She had to believe in her doctor, believe that what she was doing was for her ultimate benefit, otherwise the therapy might fail. And so it was imperative for me to change her attitude toward the "robot" she thought was her doctor.

I continued after a short pause, "Isn't she an amazing person,

Naomi?.... If you agree with me that she is truly amazing, please let me know with a nod of your head."

All responses take longer when one is in trance and I waited patiently until I noticed a tiny "yes" nod from my friend.

"Good.... That's right.... She is an amazing person.... I wonder if perhaps you didn't realize that till now.... But now that you realize it...the time has come to let her know...that you know who she really is....

"She wants you to think that she is a 'robot,' but you now know better.... People probably never say thank you to a robot.... Would you say thank you to a robot?"

She shook her head slightly in the negative. "I thought so.... I probably wouldn't tell a robot thank you either.... But now that we know she's not a robot...maybe it's time to say...'Thank you, doctor, for helping me!'....

I let her ponder that thought. She was most likely envisioning having a short conversation with the doctor, for the first time expressing her gratitude.

"Naomi, remember when your children were little...and you had to do so much for them...day and night...and they always took it for granted...and expected you to do that...and even more....When you felt that you were at the end of your rope...you probably never or almost never got a thank you from them...because they thought you just automatically...did everything for them...and you had no choice in the matter.... But you did have a choice...and you chose to put your whole heart and soul...and give up your sleep...and so many other things...to do the best for them.... And if no one ever said thank you...it must have made you feel sad...that they didn't realize how much effort you put in...for their sakes.... Wouldn't it have felt wonderful to hear, 'Thank you, Mommy'? How much did you long for those beautiful few words?"

Again, I paused, allowing the message to sink in. And then I delivered the punch line.

"Do you think, Naomi...that Dr. Sabrina would love to hear one of her patients say thank you?.... Do you think she is maybe longing for that bit of recognition?.... How good could you make her feel...if you told her how grateful you were, how much you appreciated...that she was giving up her whole life for her patients?"

The moment I made the robot in the white coat appear human in Naomi's eyes, had her understand how much Dr. Sabrina had been sacrificing for her patients—the moment I made Naomi realize that she had an obligation to relate to the doctor as a human being and express gratitude—everything would change in their relationship. I knew it would happen, because when one acts with kindness, one receives kindness in return. That's how Hashem has set up the world.[xii]

I allowed Naomi to ruminate over my words. I gave her time to imagine various scenarios in her inner world. When I felt the time was right, I continued speaking.

"Naomi, Dr. Sabrina is trying to save your life.... Would you like to make that wonderful doctor feel good?" I waited for the head nod.

"What would you like to tell her when you see her again?.... Tell me what you'd like to say to her...."

Naomi found it hard to open her mouth and articulate her words. This was a sign she was deep in trance.

The words came out slowly but clearly. "I'll tell her, 'Thank you for trying to save my life. Thanks for being so dedicated.... When do you sleep? You must be so exhausted....'"

I was thrilled with her answer. Not only did Naomi get the point that the doctor was human, not only did she understand that she really needed to express gratitude for all of the doctor's dedication, but she was actually empathizing with Dr. Sabrina over her tough daily schedule. Empathy could only breed empathy; I was sure of that.

"That's right...that's beautiful.... I'm sure she'll love to hear that coming from you.... You're going to make her day! She's going to be a much better doctor to the other patients...because you gave her a positive stroke.... She's going to love you! You'll maybe even become friends...."

I was going out on a limb here, saying things that might never happen. But I needed to exaggerate the value of what Naomi contemplated doing. In this way, I would build her motivation to actually do the deed.

The deed was still only theoretical, but it was a true beginning. As our Sages tell us, "*Sof maaseh b'machshavah techillah*—The actual deed [end product] starts in the mind."[xiii] It still needed reinforcing, and the more the better.

"I'm so proud of you, Naomi…that you are able to make Dr. Sabrina feel so good…. I'd like you to practice saying those words over and over again…. I want you to feel very sure of yourself…and at ease…when she comes in to the room…and then you'll tell her what you want to say…before she runs out…. You can even say, if you wish, 'Doctor, I'd like to tell you something'…and then she might look at you…look into your eyes…and you'll make a real connection…. So go ahead, and practice what you want to say…a few times…until the words just slide off your tongue easily…naturally…."

I gave Naomi a full five minutes to practice the scenario in her mind. Repetition is vitally important in hypnosis, as well as silence. All I had suggested up to this point was now becoming a real part of her mind as I remained silent and she relived the scene internally. This was her practice session for the real thing. Later on, her subconscious mind would enable her to carry out the task easily, almost without thinking about it.

I had actually recorded a part of our session and I intended to give Naomi the recording to listen to overnight. I felt confident that by the time she met the doctor she would be fully prepared. I was curious as to what would unfold as a result of this breakthrough. I believed that this initial conversation would merely be the tip of the iceberg in Naomi's newfound relationship with her doctor, and in her healing journey.

Naomi came out of her trance in a very mellow state. She promised to listen to the recording as often as time allowed until meeting the doctor the following day. She actually smiled when I told her, "You're so lucky Dr. Sabrina is taking care of you." Just as Sloan Kettering Hospital had been transformed, so had Dr. Sabrina Ziegler.

Being with family and visiting friends distracted me from thinking about Naomi, but the moment I was alone, my mind reverted to her and to her situation. I was exceedingly curious as to how the meeting between doctor and patient would go.

The next afternoon I was on tenterhooks until Naomi was comfortably settled in the armchair. Her treatments caused her to look pale and tired.

"How are you feeling today, Naomi?"

"Oh, OK, *baruch Hashem*. It's hard going in so often to Manhattan, but in a few days, I'll get to take a break."

"Good. I'm glad to hear that. And I'm glad that you're able to come for our sessions. How do you feel about them?"

"Our sessions? I think they're great! I think my life has turned around 180 degrees since we started!"

"What do you mean? In which way?"

"Well, first of all, my feeling toward the hospital changed. Would you believe that I now look at that building with affection? Even as I get close in the taxi and catch a glimpse of the building, I begin feeling gratitude. It's amazing!"

"Yes, it surely is. Did you see Dr. Sabrina this morning?"

"Yes."

"Tell me about it."

Naomi had a hint of a smile on her lips as she brought to mind the meeting between herself and her former nemesis. I noticed her eyes becoming wet as she relived the scene. She wiped the tears with her fingertips. I handed her a tissue.

"It was unbelievable! If someone had told me this story about Dr. Ziegler, I would not have believed it. But it happened to me." Naomi paused for breath before continuing. "The moment she walked into the room, I knew exactly what I was going to say. She was reading the chart when I said to her, 'Dr. Ziegler, I'm so glad you are my doctor. I have never seen anyone with so much dedication, so much selflessness! How do you do it?'

"She looked up slowly from the chart, a strange expression on her face. She actually peered into my eyes for the first time in all these months of treating me. I think she was stunned. Then she said, 'How nice of you to say that! I rather had the feeling that you didn't like me.'

"I felt uncomfortable, but I was happy that she was talking to me and saying something of a personal nature. So I pumped up my courage and said, 'At first I was intimidated by your style and noncommunicative nature. But then I understood it better. I realized that in order to treat as many people as possible you had to spend the minimal amount of time with each of us. So you zip in and out of each cubicle, but all for the ultimate good of your patients. When I realized all of that, I felt how hard it must be for you. No time to rest, barely time to eat, and no words of thanks from any of us. Another person would have seen what she was doing as an unbelievable burden. But you do it all as an act of kindness.'

"I stopped suddenly, afraid that I had said too much. And then I began to fear that maybe she'd be angry at me for slowing down her schedule by my silly talk. I just sat there numb. It took her quite a bit of time before she responded.

"'Mrs. Stein...,' she said. I quickly interrupted her, saying, 'My name is Naomi.' She continued, 'Naomi....' That was the first time she called me by name. 'Thank you so much for saying that. You do perceive the situation correctly and that's exactly why I have no time to talk. But this little conversation was a true gift to me. By expressing yourself to me so thoughtfully you filled me with a great feeling, giving me the justification for doing what I am doing.'

"'I'm glad, Doctor, that I was able to make you feel good. But I do hope that we will have time to talk, at least a little bit, in the future.' I looked at her pleadingly, letting her know how much I did yearn for a personal relationship with her.

"She was silent for about five seconds. This must have been a new experience for her, and she might not have known how to handle it.

Then she said, 'Yes, Naomi, I think that would be a good thing to do. It would give me something to look forward to in my long and draining day. Yes, I do think I would enjoy talking to you for a little bit whenever we meet.' She suddenly wrote something down on the chart, turned around and left the room, without a goodbye or any word at all. I think she was feeling emotional and didn't want to show it.

"I was overwhelmed with how the conversation had gone and had a little cry. I think the nurse who was attending to me was as overwhelmed as I was. She had probably never heard Dr. Ziegler say anything like that. It was a true revelation for all of us in the room, I think four people in all.

"Not only did we realize that the physician was human," she continued, "but we also began to understand how hard it is for doctors, becoming attached to their patients and then having to let go when they die. They needed to protect themselves from such overpowering emotions, otherwise they couldn't continue being doctors. I think we all got an education in those few minutes of real talk that I and Dr. Ziegler had together."

I looked at Naomi appreciatively, contemplating the transformation she had gone through in a matter of a few days. I felt an upsurge of hope as I thought about her recovery. It was clear to me that only Hashem could give Naomi a true and lasting cure, but I knew that her quality of life would be greatly enhanced by the work we had done together. And quality of life was just as important as length of days. And, of course, we had put in major *hishtadlus* for her actual physical body to heal. Time would tell if we had achieved the desired goal.

The next day was the last one Naomi and I would spend together before my return home. I used it to reinforce the changes we had achieved, in order to maximize their effects. I created numerous metaphors to solidify the messages I had implanted in her mind. I explored with her any fears, doubts, anxieties, pessimism, and any other feelings of a negative nature that she might be harboring. I treated all negative feelings as poison to her immune system, and implanted suggestions that they would no longer find a space in which to lodge within her being. They would be replaced, instead, with a variety of positive emotions. However, with the appropriate suggestions I did allow her to still feel minimal amounts of anxiety and stress, as that would enhance the intensity of her davening. I did not want her becoming passive in her *hishtadlus* for ultimate healing from the Ultimate Healer.

Naomi and I cried on each other's shoulders as we said our fare-wells. I showered her with blessings for a long and productive life, while she blessed me for the sacred work I had done with her.

Indeed, Hashem did bless her with a long and productive life. She was completely healed from the cancer and maintained her relation-ship with Dr. Ziegler for several years. She even found time in her busy schedule to speak to various women's cancer groups, giving them *chizuk* and tips for strengthening their immune systems.

What a privilege to be witness to this story.

APPENDIX A

GEDOLEI YISRAEL ON THE POWER
OF THOUGHTS AND IMAGERY

HaRav Moshe Feinstein

Note: All emphasis in bold has been added by the author.

Rav Moshe wrote in his *sefer Dorash Moshe* (introduction, p. 11):

A person who puts himself down will not reach his potential.
When you think that you will not be able to do something,
*these **thoughts prevent you** from accomplishing what you*
*really could if you **believed more** in your abilities.*

HaRav Eliyahu Dessler

Rav Dessler wrote in *Michtav Me'Eliyahu* (part IV, pp. 252–3) that
we have a powerful tool for overcoming a difficult situation. He tells
us to **imagine** ourselves going through it and succeeding, accomplishing the goal. We should imagine every possibility that might
turn up as we deal with our challenge, and imagine ourselves successfully navigating our way through each of them. **Mental imagery**
allows one to feel as though he accomplished his goal, as though he
overcame his *nisayon*. Then one can feel joy and strength from doing
it. Later on, when one is faced with the challenge, it feels as though
he has gone through it already, and he feels and knows internally
that he can succeed in his endeavor.

Maharal

The *Maharal* wrote on *Pirkei Avos* (3:18):

> We know from experience that **envisioning** a result can
> make it happen. For example, if a person apprehensively
> crosses a stream over a narrow board, the **thought** of falling
> can cause him to actually fall.

HaRav Mordechai Katz

Rav Katz wrote in his *sefer Be'er Mechokek* (pp. 105–6) about *emunah* (faith):

> It is important to **mentally visualize** the two paths that
> are before you.... When you **see this clearly** enough...this
> will become a part of your inner reality and will have **major
> ramifications** in your way of life.

APPENDIX B

NEGATIVITY

In his *sefer Shemiras Halashon* (section 4, "Laws of *Rechilus*," part 3, "Constructive Purpose"), the Chafetz Chaim writes that the trait of negativity (*nirganus*) is one of the reasons why people speak *lashon hara*. This trait is explained in *Chofetz Chaim: A Lesson A Day* (p. 331) as follows:

> *There are people who are wont to complain and find fault at every opportunity, to criticize the ways and words of their fellow, even when, in fact, he acts toward others with sincerity and has not caused them the slightest bit of harm. Such people never give others the benefit of the doubt; they assume every unintentional wrong to be deliberate, and are certain that it was done with malice. Whoever is afflicted with this terrible trait will speak lashon hora regularly, for he will view whatever others say or do as intended against himself.*
>
> *One who seeks to rid himself of this destructive trait should contemplate its various ill effects; through such reflection, he will ultimately succeed in viewing others in a favorable light.*

Hypnosis can enhance this type of reflection, which the Chafetz Chaim advises negative people to engage in, by enabling them to *see* the ill effects of this destructive trait; to *see* themselves getting rid of this trait; and to *see* the benefits in their lives by behaving in a new, positive way. Hypnosis can give them the belief that they can overcome this negative pattern, although they may have been living this way for countless years. And it can allow them to *feel*, not merely know intellectually, the joy of becoming a person of positivity.

APPENDIX C

CHOOSE POSITIVITY

Concepts for Creating Positivity

1. Seeing the cup half full or half empty is your choice.
2. Seeing the cup half full tells you, "I have." You're more likely to feel gratitude. Conversely, seeing the cup half empty emphasizes your lack. You're more likely to complain. Choose to see the blessings in your life.
3. There is always a silver lining to every cloud. Look for it.
4. You are not responsible for the thoughts that fall in, but you are responsible for what you do with them.
5. You cannot be positive and negative at the same time. Choose positivity.
6. When a negative thought enters, say, "Delete." Then reframe your thought in a positive way. The same applies to speech.
7. An obstacle can be a stumbling block, causing you to fall. It can also be a stepping stone for you to go higher. The difference is dependent on your choices.
8. You build physical muscle by lifting weights. You build spiritual muscle by overcoming adversity.
9. Hashem loves you more than you could possibly love a favorite child. He wants you to succeed. He gives you the challenges needed for your success.

10. Life, no matter what's going on, is the greatest gift. Every moment gives you opportunities for eternal happiness.

11. Desire to be and do good. From Heaven, you will be lead in that direction.

12. When Hashem gives you a challenge, He also gives you the strength to overcome it. That's a guarantee. But if you choose to enter a dangerous situation, there's no guarantee of Divine help. Pray not to be given *nisyonos*, but if they come your way from Hashem, know you will be Divinely assisted.

APPENDIX D

STRESS-MANAGEMENT TECHNIQUES

Breathe

Stress affects your health, your mood, and your body's ability to function optimally. One very effective way of reducing stress is by using breathing exercises. Your breath is a powerful tool to ease stress and make you feel less anxious and induce calm. Some simple breathing exercises can make a big difference if you make them part of your regular routine. They will help you sleep better as well.

Most people take short, shallow breaths into their chest. Breathing that way can make you feel anxious and drain your energy. With the following exercise, you will learn how to take deeper breaths, all the way into your abdomen. This type of breathing activates your vagus nerve, enhancing your relaxation even more.

1. Get comfortable. You can lie on your back in bed or on the floor with a pillow under your head and knees. Or you can sit in a chair with your shoulders, head, and neck supported against the back of the chair.
2. Breathe in through your nose. Let your belly fill with air.
3. Breathe out through your nose or mouth.
4. Place one hand on your abdomen, the other hand on your chest.
5. Breathe in and feel your abdomen rise. Breathe out, feel your abdomen lower. The hand on your abdomen should move more than the one that's on your chest.

While you do deep breathing, use a picture in your mind and a word or phrase to help you feel more relaxed.

1. Close your eyes.
2. Take a few big, deep breaths.
3. Breathe in. As you do that, imagine that the air is filled with a sensation of peace and calm. You can also imagine that your inhale has a calming color. Try to feel the color spreading throughout your body, spreading the feeling of peace and calm.
4. Breathe out. You can imagine the exhale having a color that represents stress to you. While exhaling, imagine that the stress-colored air leaves, carrying away your stress, tension, and anxiety.
5. Now use a word or phrase with your breath. As you breathe in, you can think, "I breathe in peace and calm."
6. As you breathe out, you can think, "I breathe out stress and tension."

Re-laaaax Breathing

This exercise is used to create a deep feeling of relaxation. It can alleviate anxiety, stress, worry, sadness, etc., and help you to fall asleep.

Take some deep and slow breaths, inhaling through the nose and exhaling through the mouth. Your exhale should be longer, even twice as long, as your inhale. In order to lengthen the exhale, you can form your mouth into a small circle, as though you were blowing into a balloon, making a sound as you exhale, if you wish. As you breathe in, think to yourself "*re*" and as you breathe out, think to yourself "*laaaax*."

For Hebrew speakers, you can think "*sha*" on the inhale and "*loooom*" on the exhale, or "*shal-vah*," "*ro-ga*," or "*tar-peee*."

Box Breathing

This breathing exercise is a bit more complicated. It keeps your mind focused on the breathing and off disturbing thoughts or feelings. If you feel angry, very upset, or nervous, use this breath first, and when you feel calmer, switch to the '*re-laaaax*' breathing. Box breathing is done with a very regular rhythm. It will help you feel grounded, and will give you a sense of balance, stability, a feeling of control, and will slow down your heartbeat.

Imagine a box. You inhale to a count of five as you imagine going up one side of the box. As you move across the top of the box hold your breath for a count of five. Imagine moving down the other side of the box as you exhale to a count of five. Then move across the bottom of the box holding your breath to a count of five.

Continue moving around the box again in the same way, numerous times until you feel your mood improving: inhale up the side of the box, hold breath across the top; exhale down the other side; hold breath across the bottom of the box. If breathing to a count of five is hard for you, do it to a count of four or even three, but you must maintain that rhythm throughout the exercise.

Snap the Rubber Band and Reframe

Negative thinking and speaking produces stress hormones in our body. Besides making us feel miserable, the stress hormones will tend to cause us to act in a negative way, snapping at our family members or at colleagues at work, road rage, etc. We want to create a new response to situations in life by thinking or speaking positively rather than negatively. The positive thinking and speaking will produce "happy" hormones, which will make us feel good and act more positively. At the least, this exercise will make you aware of how often you think or speak in a negative manner. It will help you to stop and rethink and rephrase.

We have tens of thousands of thoughts passing through our mind in a day, most of which we do not pay attention to. Unfortunately, most of those thoughts are negative ones. Put a rubber band on your wrist. Now, every time you catch yourself thinking or saying something negative, you pull at the rubber band and release it so that it snaps at your wrist. It's like a little slap telling you, "Stop that!" Then think of a neutral or positive way to think/say your statement. By repeatedly doing this (for as little as two weeks, although it is more effective to continue doing it for forty days), you will create a new pattern of response. You will feel much better by having lowered or eliminated stress hormones from your system.

Example: "She's late again! How disrespectful can a person be?" (*snap the rubber band*)

Reframe: "She's late. She's just very busy with everything she has to do."

Example: "It's raining and I don't have my umbrella. I'm going to get drenched!" (*snap*)

Reframe: "It's raining. Wonderful! The rain will wash the toxins out of the air!"

The Anchor

This exercise will enable you to change your state of mind from negative to positive instantly. For example, the fear of an upcoming surgery can be replaced with feelings of calm and safety.

1. Close your eyes and vividly bring to mind a powerful memory that causes feelings of joy, love, empowerment, tranquility, success, or any other very positive emotion. As you hold the memory, focus on the wonderful feelings filling you up. Try to intensify the positive feelings to their maximum.

2. When the feelings are intense, press the thumb and forefinger together of your dominant hand for ten to fifteen seconds or more. This movement is creating your anchor.

3. Open your eyes and your fingers and think some thought that completely pulls you out of the state of mind your memory put you in. For example, think of the smell of freshly popped popcorn.

4. Close your eyes and bring up the same memory again with its positive emotions. This time it might feel stronger than before. When the emotions are intense, press your fingers together to activate your anchor. Hold for some time and try

to intensify the good feelings even more. (You can imagine turning up the volume on your MP3 in order to turn up your emotions.)

5. Continue repeating numbers 3 and 4 a good number of times. You are creating a bond (anchor) in your brain between the finger movement and the positive feelings.

6. After repeating this exercise numerous times, there comes a point where you don't even have to imagine the memory in order to bring up the feelings. You simply press the fingers together and the positive feelings immediately flood your being.

The anchor exercise requires repetition in order to create new neural pathways in your brain (like creating a new habit). It is important to bring up the same memory and use the same fingers to activate the anchor. Going in and out of the memory makes it stronger and more vibrant.

You can use different memories to bring up different feelings. In this case you would create a different anchor (using different finger or fist movements) for each feeling. One memory might bring up feelings of love, another—feelings of happiness, accomplishment, or strength, etc. Each different memory with its specific feeling will be accompanied by a different anchor, i.e., touching the first and fifth fingers together; making a fist; crossing the second and third fingers, etc.

To understand this idea more fully, refer to Dr. Ivan Pavlov[xiv] and his experiment, in which he created a conditioned reflex in his dogs.

Affirmations

An affirmation is a statement that confirms something to be true. It is used in order to bring yourself to the situation that you are describing. It can be said all day long, but the best times are right upon awakening (after *modeh ani*) and before falling asleep. Commit to a minimum amount of times you will say your affirmation, but you can always say it more. Saying it out loud is better than thinking it, and saying it while looking in the mirror is even more powerful.

Repeating the affirmation repeatedly helps turn it into your new reality. For example, a very anxious person might say, *"B'siyata d'Shmaya*, from day to day I am calmer and more relaxed," while a fearful person might say, "I am stronger than I think I am."

If you feel uncomfortable making a statement that is not yet true (although you have already begun the process of bringing it about) you can say, "I choose to be/feel stronger than I think I am."

There are a few rules to keep when constructing an affirmation:

- Start with the words "I am," "I feel," or "I choose."
- Use the present tense.
- Always use positive words, never negative ones.*
- Keep it short.
- Make it specific.
- If possible, visualize an image of the changes you describe as you say the words. In that way you will engage your subconscious mind along with your conscious mind.

---

*   Do not say, for example, "From day to day, I am less and less *anxious.*" Use a positive word that is the opposite of "anxious," such as calm, relaxed, at peace, tranquil, in flow, etc.

APPENDIX E

ריפוי גוף נפש—כוחו של דמיון והיפנוזה
ההשקפה התורנית

א. כתוב בפרשת בראשית (פרק ב' פסוק ז') וייצר ד' אלוקים את האדם עפר מן
האדמה ויפח באפיו נשמת חיים ויהי האדם לנפש חיה, מגדולי תעלומות ונפלאות
הבריאה הוא היצור הנקרא אדם, אשר הקב"ה בורא ויוצר הכל חיבר וקישר בייצור
זה קשר בל ינתק של רוחניות וגשמיות כל עוד נשמת חיים בגוף ודבר זה הוא פלא
ותעלומה. קשר וחיבור זה איננו רק שהגוף הגשמי יכול לפעול בדברים רוחניים אלא גם
שביד הגשם להשפיע על הרוח וכן להיפך ביד הרוח להשפיע על הגשם. דוגמא פשוטה
לכך הוא מאמר הפסוק בתהלים (פרק ק"ד פסוק ט"ו) ויין ישמח לבב אנוש, דבר זה נ'
פשוט מרוב הרגל וכן אנו יודעים שהאלכוהול נכנס לדם וזה משפיע על האדם, אבל
בעצם דבר זה הוא פלא איך שהוא דבר גשמי יין יכול להשפיע על הרגשות שהם רוח.

ויש קשרים והשפעות בין הגוף והנפש שכל העולם יודע ומכיר בהם ואין מפקפק בדבר,
כמו שכולם יודעים שלחץ נפשי משפיע מאד על הגוף ויכול לגרום למחלות וכאבים ד'
ישמור, ואע"פ שהלחץ הוא הרגש רוחני עדיין ביכולתו להשפיע על הגוף הגשמי בכל
מיני דרכים, וכן ידוע ומפורסם גודל כח השמחה שיכול להשפיע טובות וגדולות על הגוף
להחלימו מכאביו ולרפאותו מתחלואותיו, ופסוק מפורש הוא במשלי (פרק י"ז פסוק כ"ב)
לב שמח ייטיב גהה, וכ' שם הרבינו יונה ששמחת הלב סבת רפואת האדם מחליו. ישנם
תופעות פחות ידועים לציבור הרחב אבל אנו מוצאים לזה מקורות מהתנ"ך ומחז"ל.

ב. ישנם שני כוחות נפשיים ורוחניים היכולים להשפיע פיזית על הגוף, הא' הוא ע"י
רגשות שונות כמו רגשות שמחה עצבות כעס וכד', והשני הוא ע"י כח הדמיון ומחשבה.
ויש פסוקים מפורשים בתנ"ך על השפעת הרגשות על הגוף, במשלי (פרק ט"ו פסוק
ל') כתוב שמועה טובה תדשן עצם, ועוד פסוק במשלי (פרק י"ז פסוק כ"ב) ורוח נכאה
תיבש גרם, עיי"ש במפרשים, ועוד פסוק במשלי (פרק ט"ו פסוק י"ג) לב שמח ייטיב
פנים, וכ' שם הרבינו יונה וז"ל, נתכוון שלמה ע"ה שנלמוד מזה שלא יעלה על הדעת

שאין תועלת והפסד על מחשבות הלב כי אם בדברים ובפועל ונתן מופת כי יש ללב פועל בגוף כי עיקר הנאת הגוף וצערו תלויים בלב עכ"ל.

ידוע המעשה המסופר בגמ' במסכת גיטין דף נ"ו עמוד ב' שרי"ח בן זכאי הגיע לשר הצבא של רומי שעמד לכבוש את ירושלים ולאחר שלבש נעל א' הגיע אליו השמועה שמינו אותו לקיסר ולא הצליח ללבוש את הנעל השניה וגם לא הצליח להוריד את הנעל שכבר לבש, ורי"ח בן זכאי אמר לו שזה בגלל שמועה טובה ששמע, והציע פתרון שיביאו לפניו אדם אשר שונא וכך עשה והצליח ללבוש את הנעל השניה.

ג. וכן יש לנו מקור מהתו' על גודל השפעתו של כח המחשבה והדמיון על הגוף, והוא מעשה המקלות שיעקב אבינו שם לפני הצאן, שע"י שהצאן ראו צבעים מסוימים הם ילדו וולדות בצבע שונה מטבעם ע"י כח הציור והדמיון, המדרש רבה בפר' ויצא פרשה ע"ג פסקא י' מביא סיפור שמוסיף להדגיש את כח הדמיון וז"ל, מעשה בכושי אחד שנשא לכושית אחת והוליד ממנה בן לבן תפס האב לבן ובא לו אצל ר' א"ל שמא אינו בני א"ל היה לך מראות בתוך ביתך א"ל הן א"ל שחורה או לבנה א"ל לבנה א"ל מיכן שהיה לך בן לבן ע"כ. הרי מלמדים אותנו חז"ל שבכח הציור המחשבה והדמיון בהמות יכולות להוליד וולדות השונות מהן בצבען, וכן איש ואשה כושים יכולים להוליד בן לבן.

ועי' באגרות הקודש לרמב"ן פ"ה שהאריך בעניינים גדולים ונפלאים כמה עצמה ורב שפע יש בכח המחשבה והדמיון, וע"ע מה שביאר הרמב"ן ז"ל בעניין נחש הנחושת בבמדבר פר' חוקת פרק כ"א פסוק ט'.

ה. לכל אדם יש שני שכלים השכל המודע והשכל התת מודע, תפקידו של השכל המודע הוא כח השיפוט והעיון וכל מה שאנו רגילים לקרוא שכל, ותפקידו של השכל התת מודע הוא לפעול בצורה אוטומטית ובלתי שיפוטית כמו רפלקסים ואינסטינקטים וכדו', וכן הרבה דברים הם בסמכות של השכל התת מודע. יש מעלה וחסרון למודע ולתת מודע אבל האדם צריך את שניהם כדי לחיות. הרופאים אומרים שמה שהאדם שמע וראה כל ימי חייו מיום היוווצרו חקוקים בשכל התת מודע אלא שלפעמים לשכל המודע אין גישה לכל אותם אוצרות חבויים. בהיפנוזה מביאים את האדם למצב של כעין חצי תרדמה, ובמצב זה יש גישה לשכל התת מודע, מומחי היפנוזה וכן רופאים ופסיכולוגים משתמשים בהיפנוזה ככלי לגלות סיבות חבויים לקשיים נפשיים או מחלות, ואז מנווטים את השכל התת מודע לנטרל בעיות אלו ע"י כח הדמיון והמחשבה.

ה. גישתה ההשקפתית של אמי מורתי תליט"א בכל עניינים אל, שהבורא ית' הוא כל יכול ורק הוא רופא כל בשר ואין היא אלא שליח מאת הקב"ה, והתפקיד שלה זה לעזור לאנשים ע"י הידע הנרחב שרכשה במשך עשרות שנים, ולגלות להם דרכים נוספות לבד מהרפואה הקונבנציונלית, וכבר אמרו חז"ל (ירושלמי כתובות פי"ג ה"ב) שלא מן הכל אדם זוכה להתרפאות, ולפעמים ע"י הידע הנרחב שלה היא הצינור והשליח של הקב"ה לעזור לפציינט מסויים.

ו. ולעניין הלכה אם מותר להתרפאות ע"י היפנוזה ודמיון מודרך ודברים מעין אלו,
כבר הורה היתר הגאון בעל הערוך לנר בשו"ת בנין ציון סי' ס"ז לעניין היפנוזה, וכן
בשו"ת אגרות משה יו"ד ח"ב סי' מ"ה, ובשו"ת עשה לך רב ח"ה סי' י"ג. אינני יכול
לדבר ולהעיד על דרכים שונות ומגוונות של רפואות הקיימות היום, אבל בכל מה
שקשור לשיטות שאמי מורתי משתמשת הדבר פשוט להיתר כי אין כאן שימוש
בכוחות סגוליים כלחשים וכד', אלא נסיון להשפיע על הגוף בכח המחשבה והדמיון.

ז. הלב ידווה על זה שהרבה האנשים והרופאים וכן הרבה רבנים אינם מודעים לנושא
של רפואת גוף נפש, ומה נורא המחזה על אנשים ששפכו את כל הונם ויותר מכך וכתתו
רגליהם שנים ע"ג שנים מרופא לרופא למצוא מזור למחלתם, ורק כאשר התייאשו לגמרי
ובעיניהם כלו כל הקיצים החליטו לנסות את הגישה של רפואת גוף נפש ועד מהרה אירע
להם הנס הגדול להם יחלו והתפללו הם וכל משפחתם שנים ע"ג שנים. במשך השנים
שמעתי מאמי מורתי תליט"א סיפורים מדהימים על רפואות וישועות, אבל לא אהיה עד
מפי עד אלא בדידי הוה עובדא, הכרנו משפחה שהאשה ילדה כמה ילדים והנה עצר ד'
בעד רחמה ובמשך כמה שנים לא ילדה, הפנינו את האשה לאמי מורתי תליט"א ולאחר
כמה טיפולים נכנסה האשה להריון, כפי ששמענו מהמטופלת והמטפלת שהאשה עברה
איזה קושי נפשי גדול באמצע החיים וזה היה השליח של הקב"ה לעצור אותה מללדת,
ולאחר שהבעיה טופלה נכנסה להריון וילדה בחסדי ד' ית'.
בברכה

דוד הלוי טופורוביץ, מחבר "דברי משה"

בעניין השפעת המחשבה על הגוף פיזית, אינני מבין בדברים האלו, אבל כבר מצינו אצל
יעקב אבינו ששם מקלות בשקתות המים, וכתוב במדרש תנחומא פרשת נשא, מעשה
במלך הערביים ששאל את רבי עקיבא אני כושי ואשתי כושית וילדה לי בן וכי'
ואמר לו ר"ע שנתנה עיניה בצורה לבנה, ואם תמה אתה בדבר למד מן צאנו של יעקב
שמן המקלות היו מתיחמות, והודה מלך הערביים ושבח לר' עקיבא, וברמב"ן פרשת
חקת כתב, מפלאות התולדה כי נשוך הכלב השוטה אחרי שנשתטה בחליו אם יקובל
השתן שלו בכלי זכוכית יראה בשתן דמות גורי כלבים קטנים ואם תעביר המים במטלית
ותסננם לא תמצא בהם שום רושם כלל וכשתחזיר לכלי הזכוכית וישתהו שם כשעה
תחזור ותראה שם גורי הכלבים מתוארים, וכתב שזה אמת הוא בפלאי כחות הנפש.
בברכה

ישראל הלוי טופורוביץ, מחבר ספר "דרך ישראל"
וראש כולל "עמל התורה" אחיסמך, ורב קהילת "חזון איש"
אחיסמך ובית שמש, ורב בית הכנסת "אהל לאה" בית שמש.

ENDNOTES

i   Sudden Infant Death Syndrome (SIDS) is the unexplained death, usually during sleep, of a seemingly healthy baby less than a year old. SIDS is sometimes known as crib death because the infants often die in their cribs.

ii   *Shemiras Halashon, "Shaar Hazechirah,"* perek 2; *Megillah* 12b.

iii   Dr. Domar, executive director of the Domar Center for Mind/Body Health, is a pioneer in the application of mind-body medicine to infertility care and author of *Conquering Infertility: Dr. Alice Domar's Mind/Body Guide to Enhancing Fertility and Coping with Infertility.*

iv   *Tehillim* 91:15.

v   Emotional Freedom Technique (EFT), or "tapping," is a method widely publicized by Gary Craig in the 1990s. Relief of a wide range of physical and emotional issues is achieved by tapping on meridian energy points.

vi   Rabbi Yisroel Zev Gustman (1908–1991), a Talmudic genius, a rabbi, and the last rabbinic judge in Vilna during World War II.

vii   Dr. Milton Erickson, American psychiatrist (1901–1980), specializing in medical hypnosis. He created "indirect hypnosis."

viii   Dr. Candace Pert, American internationally recognized neuroscientist (1946–2013), author of *Molecules of Emotion.*

ix   Dr. Carl Simonton, American radiation oncologist (1942–2009), treating cancer in the 1970s. His pioneering work with the mind-body connection between health and illness utilized imagery to harness the patient's positive energy. He founded the Simonton Center and coauthored *Getting Well Again.*

x   Dr. Bernie Siegel, American retired pediatric surgeon and writer (b. 1932), he is an internationally recognized expert in the field of cancer treatment and complementary, holistic medicine. He writes and teaches about mind-body medicine and the relationship between the patient and the healing process. In 1978, he founded Exceptional Cancer Patients (ECaP). He authored *Love, Medicine and Miracles.*

xi   Memorial Sloan Kettering Cancer Center is located in Manhattan, New York City. Founded in 1884, it is the world's oldest and largest private cancer center, providing patient care, innovative research, educational programs, clinical studies, and treatment.

xii   See endnote ii.

xiii   In the *Lechah Dodi* prayer said upon the onset of Shabbos.

xiv   In the 1890s, Russian physiologist Ivan Pavlov conducted research on salivation in dogs in response to being fed. He was able to cause his dogs to salivate when they heard a sound they associated with their meat being brought to them. This is known as a "conditioned reflex."

BIBLIOGRAPHY

Erickson, Milton H. *Healing in Hypnosis*.
  Irvington Publishers, 1983.

Gordon, Marilyn. *Extraordinary Healing*.
  Wise Word Publishing, 2000.

Hogan, Kevin. *The New Hypnotherapy Handbook*.
  Morris Publishing, 1961.

Naparstek, Belleruth. *Staying Well with Guided Imagery*.
  Warner Books, 1994.

Rossman, Martin. *Healing Yourself*.
  Walker Publishing Company, 1987.

Siegel, Bernie. *Love, Medicine and Miracles*.
  Harper Collins Publishers, 1990.

GLOSSARY

ad meah v'esrim shanah

    lit., "until 120 years"; an expression used to denote "until the end of a person's life."

aliyas neshamah   elevation for the soul.

almanah   widow.

apikores   heretic; disbeliever.

avodas Hashem   service of G-d.

b'chasdei Hashem   by (acts of) G-d's loving-kindness.

b'ezras Hashem   with G-d's help.

b'siyata d'Shmaya   with Heavenly assistance.

badeken   the act of covering the bride's face by the groom before the marriage ceremony.

bar mitzvah   a thirteen-year-old Jewish boy; the day a Jewish boy turns thirteen and takes on the yoke of mitzvah observance.

baruch Hashem   blessed be G-d.

bayis ne'eman b'Yisrael

    lit., "a loyal home in Israel"; a blessing said to new couples ("May you establish a *bayis ne'eman b'Yisrael*").

beis din   a Jewish house of law.

berachah (pl.–berachos)

> a blessing recited over food or drink or when doing a commandment; a blessing for good to be bestowed upon the listener.

bitachon	trust (in G-d).
Borei Olam	Creator of the world.
chagim	Jewish holidays.
chassan	a bridegroom or fiancé.
Chassidic	of or relating to Chassidim and their way of life.
chas v'shalom	G-d forbid.
Chazal	an acronym for *chachameinu zichronam li'verachah*, "our Sages of blessed memory."
chessed	an act of loving-kindness.
chizuk	strength; encouragement.
Chol Hamoed	the intermediary days of Pesach or Sukkos.
chuppah	a wedding canopy, under which the religious marriage ceremony takes place.
daas Torah	Torah viewpoint or truth, articulated by a Torah scholar.
dan l'chaf zechus	giving the benefit of the doubt; judging favorably.
daven	pray.
emunah	faith.
Eretz Yisrael	the land of Israel.
Gemara	(a volume of) Talmud.
halachah	Jewish law.
halachic/halachically	referring to Jewish law.
Hashem	G-d.

hashkafah	Jewish philosophy.
hashkafic	relating to Jewish philosophy.
hishtadlus	effort.
Igros Hakodesh	lit., "the holy letters"; a book written by Nachmanides.
Kabbalah	Jewish mysticism.
kallah	a bride; a fiancée.
kever	a grave.
kollel	Torah institute of learning for married men who are supported by a monetary stipend.
korban	a sacrifice; a scapegoat.
Kosel	the Western Wall or Wailing Wall (also called Kosel Maaravi), the holiest Jewish prayer site.
l'havdil elef havdalos	lit., "to differentiate a thousand differentiations"; an expression meaning to differentiate very greatly between things, people, or situations
levayah	funeral.
lo sitor	the Jewish commandment, "You shall not bear a grudge."
lashon hora	derogatory or damaging speech about others.
malach/malachim	angel/s.
mashgiach	spiritual supervisor or guide; a rabbi within a yeshiva responsible for the non-academic areas of yeshiva students' lives.
mazal tov	lit., "good constellation (fate)"; congratulations.
Midrash Rabbah	written by Rabbi David Adani (Yemen, fourteenth century); can refer to part of or the collective whole of specific Aggadic

	expositions; Biblical interpretation prominent in the Talmudic literature.
Midrash Tanchuma	the name given to three different collections of Biblical Aggadah (eighth or ninth century).
mekubal/mekubalim	mystic/s versed in Kabbalah.
meshuga'as	craziness.
Mishlei	the book of Proverbs.
mitzvah	Torah commandment.
modeh ani	Jewish prayer upon awakening, thanking G-d for a new day of life.
navi	prophet.
neshamah	soul.
netilas yadayim	Jewish ritual of washing the hands upon rising in the morning, before eating bread, etc.
niftar	dead person; died.
nirganus	negativity.
nisyonos	challenges; tests; travails.
olam ha'emes	the world of truth; the afterlife.
Parashas	the Torah portion of.
Perek Shirah	lit., "Chapter of Song"; nature's song of thanks, attributed to King David, in which all the components of Creation sing their own praises of their Maker.
Pirkei Avos	Ethics of the Fathers.
rabbanim	rabbis; educators.
rabbeim	rabbis, educators.
Rabbeinu Yonah	Rabbi Jonah ben Abraham Gerondi, a rabbi and moralist, most famous for his ethical work *The Gates of Repentance*.

Ramban	Rabbi Moshe ben Nachman, commonly known as Nachmanides.
Rashbi	Rabbi Shimon bar Yochai.
rav	rabbi.
rebbetzin	rabbi's wife; an authoritative female involved in Jewish education.
roga	peace; calm.
seder	slot of time allotted to the learning schedule in yeshiva.
sefer	book; Jewish religious book.
segulos	plural for "remedy" or "protection"; a protective or benevolent charm or ritual in Kabbalistic and Talmudic tradition.
seudas hodaah	thanksgiving feast.
Shabbos	the Sabbath.
shaliach	messenger.
shalom	peace; a greeting for hello and goodbye.
shalvah	peace of mind; calm.
Shavuos	Jewish holiday of Pentecost.
shidduch/shidduchim	matchmaking proposal/s; loosely used to mean a match in any endeavor.
Shlomo HaMelech	King Solomon.
shalom bayis	marital and/or domestic harmony.
shamayim	heaven; sky.
shul	synagogue.
simchahs	plural for happiness; a joyous occasion; a celebration.
siyata d'Shmaya	Heavenly assistance.
sukkah	booth built on the holiday of Sukkos.

tafkid	duty; task; personal mission.
tahor	pure.
talmid chacham	Torah scholar.
tarpee	relax.
tefillah	prayer.
Tehillim	the book of Psalms; chapters from the book of Psalms.
tikkun	atonement; rectification.
tzarah	trouble; distress; suffering.
Yaakov Avinu	our father (forebear) Jacob.
yahrtzeits	plural of the anniversary of the Jewish calendar date on which someone passed away.
Yekke	a Jew of German-speaking origin. The term, which carries the connotation that German Jews pay great attention to detail and punctuality, is also used to describe people with those characteristics.
Yerushalmi	Jerusalem Talmud; a person originating from or living in Jerusalem.
yeshiva	Jewish educational institution that focuses on the study of traditional religious texts, primarily the Talmud and the Torah.
yeshiva gedolah	yeshiva for young men aged seventeen and above.
yeshua/yeshuos	salvation/s.
yetzer hara	the evil inclination.
Yirmiyahu HaNavi	the prophet Jeremiah.
zocheh	to merit.

ABOUT THE AUTHOR

Bracha Pearl Toporowitch, wife, mother, grandmother, and great-grandmother, was born in London, England. She grew up in Brooklyn, and her high school years were spent under the tutelage of Rebbetzin Vichna Kaplan, *a"h*. After her marriage, she lived in Lakewood, New Jersey, during the time Rav Shneur Kotler, *zt"l*, was Rosh Yeshiva, and then she made aliyah with her family. She currently lives in Zichron Yaakov in the north of Israel. She has been working with women in various capacities since 1969, and since 1999 as a guided imagery practitioner and hypnotherapist. In 2017, she opened the Mind-Body Healing Fertility Clinic in Ramat Beit Shemesh, Israel. Mrs. Toporowitch gives *shiurei Torah* in Hebrew and English and always weaves true Jewish *hashkafah* into her work as a practitioner.

Mrs. Toporowitch was personally affected by the disastrous Egged Bus number 2 suicide bombing in August 2003—dubbed by the media as "the children's bus bombing"—as some of her close family members were on that bus. She gleaned many lessons for life from that traumatic event, which she continues to publicize in her speeches and writings.

She is the author of *At Your Command* (Targum, 2008), the riveting account of the life of her father; *From Darkness to Dawn* (Mosaica Press, 2018), the first novel of the Perlman family saga; and *Sparks of Radiance* (Mosaica Press, 2020), the second novel of the Perlman family saga.